DAN JENKINS'
TEXAS COLLEGE ★ FOOTBALL LEGENDS

JOHN DAVID CROW

Heart *of a* Champion

BY STEVE PATE

EDITED BY
DAN JENKINS

M
SPORTS

IN ASSOCIATION WITH THE
Fort Worth Star-Telegram

Fort Worth Star-Telegram

Wesley R. Turner, President and Publisher
Michael Blackmon, Vice President, Editorial Director
Jack B. Tinsley, Vice President, Community Affairs
Jim Witt, Vice President, Executive Editor
Kevin Dale, Managing Editor

Acknowledgements

All chapters in the "Ten to Remember" section are reprinted
by permission of the *Fort Worth Star-Telegram*. Copyright © 1955, 1956 and 1957
by the *Fort Worth Star-Telegram*. All rights reserved.

Designed by Lori Leath-Smith

ISBN 1-57028-165-3
ISBN (Leatherbound Edition) 1-57028-176-9

Published by

Masters Press
2647 Waterfront Parkway, East Drive
Indianapolis, Indiana 46214
317-298-5706

For other sports publications in the Masters Press library,
call toll-free 1-800-722-2677 or contact our web site at www.masterspress.com

CONTENTS

Crow & Jenkins: Two Unforgettable Texans

Rain, hail, 90-mph wind and one tough football player. Well, there were actually two teams of tough football players, but there was only one John David Crow. And, unfortunately for TCU, he played for Texas A&M.

It was the famed "Hurricane Game" of 1956. While the Aggies and the Horned Frogs were beating on each other, Mother Nature decided to get in the game. The game matched TCU's potent offense and A&M's rock-solid defense against Nature's best obstacles.

Crow was a fierce athlete who defined Paul (Bear) Bryant's notion of a football player. He was a vicious hitter at linebacker and delivered as much punishment when he carried the ball on offense.

Crow's performance on both sides of the line earned him a spot in Dan Jenkins' Texas College Football Legends series. The series will include profiles of a dozen players and coaches who have shaped college football in a state that has been producing Saturday afternoon thrills for decades.

"Bryant coached a lot of great players over the years," Crow told The Fort Worth Star-Telegram in 1993, "but you didn't really have to be some kind of blue-chip talent, necessarily. His type of player was ... well, I won't say you had to be a farm boy, but you had to have a toughness about you, that's what he was looking for."

Bryant found it in Crow. In 1957, Crow turned his talent into A&M's only Heisman Trophy winner.

But back to Oct. 20, 1956 — and the rain. TCU had the ball on the Aggies' 3-yard line. TCU's famed back, Jim Swink, slammed into the line. The officials spotted the ball an inch from the end zone. On fourth down,

Swink hit the line again. The Aggie defense held, according to the officials. TCU fans disagree to this day.

"I had a real good vantage point," Crow told The Star-Telegram in defense of the call. "I was on the bottom of the pile at the goal line."

In the second half, Crow started an Aggie offensive drive with a 21-yard sweep. After A&M moved to the TCU eight-yard line, Crow caught the Aggies' lone pass of the day for a touchdown.

The game sums up Crow's status in Texas football lore. He was the prototype player for the rugged coach. After college, Crow played professional football with the Cardinals and 49ers. He had two 1,000-yard rushing seasons and was named All-Pro.

He never lost his bond with Bryant. After his playing career ended, Crow coached with Bryant at Alabama and sent his son to play for the Bear. He then returned to A&M, rising to become athletic director.

"If it hadn't been for him," Crow said of Bryant, "I might have spend most of my life back in Springhill, (La.), throwing stuff off of boxcars."

Dan Jenkins was a sportswriter when Crow was terrorizing Southwest Conference opponents. Jenkins is synonymous with football in Texas. He grew up in Fort Worth, watching his beloved TCU Horned Frogs. When he decided to turn his attention to chronicling those Saturday afternoon feats, the sports world became a better place.

Southwest Conference football spoke to Jenkins, and he translated for the rest of us.

Kevin Dale
Managing Editor
Fort Worth Star-Telegram

Mighty John David

By Dan Jenkins

You sort of face a problem when you try to talk about John David Crow—there are no stats to work with. They didn't keep stats on the number of people he trampled when he lugged the football for Bear Bryant's spirited Texas Aggies.

Last time I looked, they were still digging guys up out of the turf in numerous stadiums around Texas that used to be part of the Southwest Conference. John David had been there.

Bear Bryant said it first, of course.

When Crow became the third Southwest Conference player to win the Heisman Trophy in 1957 — following TCU's Davey O'Brien in '38 and SMU's Doak Walker in '48 — a sportswriter said to Bryant:

"Coach, John David only gained 562 yards from scrimmage. That's not many yards for a Heisman winner."

To which Bear calmly replied, "That don't count all the people he knocked down."

Truer words were never spoken, especially by a football coach.

John David Crow, the pride of Springhill, La., was about as good a tough-yardage runner as ever slipped into a football suit, maroon and white or otherwise. A roaring, rock-hard 6-2 and 218, he was slashing, churning, barging ball carrier.

You wanted five yards in a dire situation, John David was your man.

And that says nothing about the way he could turn a five-yard pass catch into a steamrolling 20-yard gain. Or how he could pulverize an opponent with a crushing block. Or how his bone-rattling tackles when he played defense could quickly turn a baritone into a soprano.

As Bear often remarked to various groups of sportswriters, myself included, when he was campaigning for Crow to win the Heisman in '57, "It's those things you

fellows don't notice that make John David a complete football player — one of the greatest I ever hope to see."

It has long since passed into legend that Crow was so good, he was the only one of Bryant's many stars at Kentucky, Texas A&M, and Alabama that Bear called by his first name.

Such immortals as Joe Namath, Lee Roy Jordan, and Babe Parilli were known to Bear as "Namath," "Jordan," and "Parilli," on the practice field, but Crow was always addressed as "John David."

Coming from Bryant himself, that alone might say more about the rugged Aggie halfback than anything else.

In a way, John David was Jarrin' John Kimbrough revisited on the maroon and white.

They were similar in size and ball-carrying style — knees high, barreling over folks. Both were modest and uassuming. And both led their Texas A&M teams to starling success in their separate eras.

Kimbrough was a two-time all-American and runnerup for the Heisman, a destructive fullback who led the Aggies to a national championship as a junior in '39 and a near-No. 1 as a senior in '40.

Crow was the all-American halfback and Heisman winner who burned the seasons of 1956 and '57 into the soul of every Aggie and Soutwest Conference follower as he guided A&M to a couple of near-No. 1 seasons.

In fact, in 1956 John David took the Aggies to a 9-0-1 record, their first undefeated season since the Kimbrough team of '39, which wound up 11-0 after the Sugar Bowl.

John David would be the first to say he had a lot of help on that '56 Aggie team. He was joined by guys like Jack Pardee, Charlie Krueger, Dennis Goehring, Don Watson, Lloyd Hale, Roddy Osborne, Gene Stallings and a few others. Guys who, two years earlier, had gone to Junction, Tex., and lived to tell about it.

Although the '56 team wound up No. 5 in most polls, I like to make the case that those Aggies were more deserving of No. 1 than anyone else. After the bowl games, Texas A&M and Oklahoma were the only unbeaten teams left in the country, but Bryant's Cadets had played far tougher opponents.

Oklahoma was 10-0 against a schedule of teams that won only 32 games and included only one foe with a winning record, that being Colorado. Meanwhile, John David and the Aggies faced teams that rang up 49 victories!

Moreover, five of those rivals had winning records, and a couple of them, TCU and Baylor, were the among the nation's heavyweights. TCU and Baylor had fallen to the Aggies in classic, storybook, legendary games during the regular season, but later on it was TCU that beat No. 8 Syracuse — and halfback Jim Brown — by 28-27 in the Cotton Bowl, and Baylor that upset No. 2 Tennessee — and tailback Johnny Majors — by 13-7 in the Sugar Bowl.

Pardon me now while I slip in a slice of history regarding the lusty old Southwest Conference, which after 80 years fell victim to modern greed. It relates to John David Crow, anyhow. Shows you what company he kept.

It so happens that only 20 teams that played a representative schedule, out of all those years, managed to get through a regular season undefeated. Here they are along with their most notable player, for ID purposes:

1926 — SMU, 8-0-1 (Gerald Mann)
1927 — Texas A&M, 8-0-1 (Joel Hunt)
1929 — TCU, 9-0-1 (Cy Leland)
1932 — TCU, 10-0-1 (Johnny Vaught)
1935 — SMU, 12-0 (Bobby Wilson)
1938 — TCU, 10-0 (Davey O'Brien)
1939 — Texas A&M, 10-0 (John Kimbrough)
1947 — SMU, 9-0-1 (Doak Walker)
1956 — Texas A&M, 9-0-1 (John David Crow)
1962 — Texas, 9-0-1 (Ernie Koy)
1963 — Texas, 10-0 (Tommy Nobis)
1964 — Arkansas, 10-0 (Ken Hatfield)
1965 — Arkansas, 10-0 (Jon Brittenum)
1969 — Texas, 10-0 (James Street)
1970 — Texas, 10-0 (Steve Worster)
1977 — Texas, 11-0 (Earl Campbell)
1982 — SMU, 10-0-1 (Eric Dickerson)
1983 — Texas, 11-0 (Jerry Gray)
1992 — Texas A&M, 12-0 (Greg Hill)
1994 — Texas A&M, 10-0-1 (Leeland McElroy)

John David (44) outraces St. Louis Cardinals defensive back Jerry Stovall on a deep route.

Speaking of A&M's games against TCU and Baylor in '56 they came back-to-back on the schedule in October, and you would be hard-pressed to name a college outfit that ever faced two tougher opponents on successive Saturday.

TCU with all-American Jim Swink came to College Station on Oct. 20 with a 3-0 record, having mauled Kansas, Arkansas and Alabama. The Horned Frogs were

looked like touchdowns to TCU fans but no-gain to Aggie fans as well as the game officials.

The Aggies finally yielded a touchdown pass in the third quarter and trailed, 6-0, with little time left in the game, but that's when John David went to work. His bolting 21-yard run ignited the 80-yard drive that won the game. It was another of his jarring runs that carried the Aggies down to the TCU 8-yard. There, John David took an option pass from the other halfback, Don Watson, and barreled over for one of the most precious touchdowns of his career. Little Loyd Taylor's placekick then provided the difference.

When the Bear was asked afterward if the game had gone according to his defensive plan, he said, "No, it went according to prayer."

It was then on Oct. 27, one hectic week later, that the Aggies were in Waco confronting a 4-0 Baylor team, a group of Bears led by the swift Del Shofner that were fresh from whipping California, Texas Tech, Maryland, and Arkansas and were now in the nation's Top 10 themselves.

Bryant would later refer to that Baylor contest as "the bloodiest, meanest, toughest game I ever saw." The Bears dominted it and were leading until late in the fourth quarter when Mr. John David Crow once again came to the rescue. He rumbled six yards on fourth down for the touchdown that gave A&M a 19-13 victory.

It's safe to say that John David's heroics in those two clutch games gave him a pretty good start on the Heisman he won a year later.

Not long ago I found myself in a delightful gathering of Heisman winners, one of whom was John David. Naturally, we found ourselves — an old Horned Frog and and old Aggie — reliving some treasured Southwest Conference moments.

It was during the course of our visit that I couldn't resist saying, "Swink scored, you know."

He burst out laughing, and said, "He did not! I was right there!"

Then we both started laughing at something else — the fact that we were talking about a game that was played 40 years ago.

Only in college football.

Which is why you never forget a John David Crow.

ranked No. 3 in the nation and were feverish to get revenge for a heartbreaking 19-16 loss to John David and the Aggies in '55, their only defeat of the regular season.

This was the famous "hurricane game" at Kyle Field. Only Bryant's defensive scheme and the Aggies who played it so fiercely kept A&M from being swept off the field for three quarters. Five times the Frogs drove inside A&M's 5-yard line but failed to score, including two controversial plunges by Swink from the Aggies' 1-yard line during the second quarter tornado, a couple of stabs that

An Aggie Legend

CHAPTER ONE

A Difficult Road to Glory

The albatross hanging around John David Crow's neck the day he was born happened to be his own umbilical cord.

Velma Crow was 26 and had already given birth to two healthy children. The town doctor assured her a midwife could easily handle delivery. Just send word, he said, and he'd drop by to check up on mama and the newborn.

But in sweltering Louisiana heat on July 8, 1935, in the bedroom of the Crows' modest home in Marion, as Velma's pushing and grunting and howling subsided, the midwife found herself staring at a 10-pound boy whose navel cord – as the umbilical was known in the country – strangled his little throat like an octopus' tentacles.

Frantically, the midwife untwisted the 18-inch cord, but the snarled, slippery rope had retarded blood flow to the head.

Later, the doctor said the nerves on the left side of the face were too badly damaged, explaining the deep vertical crease, and why the left corner of the baby's mouth slumped downward in an exaggerated frown, and why one eye would always look sleepier than the other.

Throughout John David Crow's boyhood and most of his early adult life, the face would bear this frozen expression, the mouth slurring off to one side, the left eyelid somewhere between half open, half shut. He could not keep the eye completely closed, even when sleeping.

But Velma and Harry Crow were not about to make their new son feel freakish by treating him any differently than the others. Pampering was never all that fashionable in Louisiana anyway.

Harry was a big, tough, chiseled man, 6-1, 240, not given to book-learning. A ferocious inner drive helped him deal with the Great Depression and other hard times as a farmer would a fly, with a shooing swat of the hand. If he ever owned a dictionary, the word "coddle" was not in it.

In July 1997, on one of the handful of days sandwiched between his 43rd wedding anniversary and 62nd birthday, John David leaned back in his chair in his Rudder Tower office on Texas A&M's sprawling campus, and probably sounded a great deal like his own gray-haired dad when he said of his palsy-like facial paralysis: "I wouldn't say it haunted me or was a major handicap in my life ... at times I suppose it was a minor inconvenience."

That same day, from their fashionable two-story home in a new country club subdivision 10 miles southwest of the A&M campus, Carolyn Crow mentioned her husband's physical defect only within the context of ex-

John David at age 4

plaining his love affair with football. They had been high school sweethearts for six months before marrying in the summer of 1954, when they threw all they owned into the backseat of a car and lit out on a course that would take them to College Station then, as teenagers, and again 29 years later.

You will find Carolyn's fingerprints all over her husband's 1957 Heisman Trophy, his college degree, his 11-year professional playing career, and everything else he would accomplish.

Football provided some mighty waves in the voyage that has been John David's life, but the former Carolyn Gilliam has always provided the ocean.

She had been Miss Springhill (La.), Miss Lumberjack, "the prettiest gal in the state" in the eyes of John David (and, likely others).

The day following their 43rd anniversary, she said, "You know? John David and I never talked about football while he was playing, but I've always known how important it is to him. With the birth defect he had growing up, he could have withdrawn, and he probably would have missed out on a lot had it not been for athletics.

"I think that's why football was always uniquely his, rather than something he shared with me and most others. I've known a lot of players' and coaches' wives, and some don't like the game, but I would have never interfered with John David's love for anything that gave him back so much in return."

In the 1940's, football was the last thing on the minds of Velma and Harry Crow, even after their oldest boy, Raymond, brought the sport up a few times at the supper table. Five years John David's senior, Raymond broke the ice for his little brother by withstanding their father's verbal tirades. Harry ranted against the game, consid-

"I can't stand the thought of you getting hurt," she said, trying to soothe John David's frustration. "We can't afford any broken bones around here anyway."

Velma Crow

ered it a silly waste of a boy's time, and forbid Raymond from going out in junior high. Why on earth would anyone spend all those hours horsing around in a cow pasture when he could be earning honest money on the job? It simply made no sense.

Raymond went out anyway. Secretly. He limped home injured one day, expecting wrath. But when Raymond convinced his dad he'd still like to play, that all his pals did, Harry relented.

By then, the Crows were living in Springhill, Harry having accepted a transfer to the International Paper Company. Springhill was another small town, two Louisiana parishes to the northwest of Marion, near the Arkansas border. They were lucky to be taking John David along: as a 2-year-old, he almost died of pneumonia. The doctor sat down with Velma and Harry and suggested they brace themselves; and, they continued to closely monitor John David's health even after their prayers went answered.

He always looked so frail, so raw-boned. He never seemed to eat as much as Raymond or the older girl, Doris Ann. Even little Yvonne, now the youngest of four children, scraped her plates cleaner.

During John David's grade-school years, Harry and Velma did some research and started John on a daily regimen of vitamin pills. John studied up on his own and got wind that nothing fills out a boy like bananas. He ate 'em whole, sliced them into his cereal, and mashed them into peanut-butter sandwiches.

Little John David did not seem to be making much headway in the classroom either. His second-grade teacher blamed it on immaturity, and a complete lack of attentiveness. She confided to Velma that John seemed far more preoccupied staring out the window than at the blackboard. His parents and the second-grade teacher decided to hold him back a year, forcing him to repeat the grade he had just passed.

But the decision proved to be a blessing. John had been the youngest in his class because of his July birthday. Repeating the second grade placed him with children a little younger or his own age.

Despite the early fretting and schoolhouse evaluations, John David was expected to be just as tough-minded and stoic as the rest of the Crows. These traits came deeply rooted in the family tree, and Harry determinedly ingrained them into his four children, like a gardener watering his plants so they will blossom at the right time.

Harry was a man of few words and fewer compliments. The love he had for his children, more certain than turkey on Thanksgiving, did not require vocal reminders.

Velma showed a softer side, but she understood how

important it was for her sons to put away childish things as soon as possible. The only time she felt compelled to protect John David was the day he tried out for football as a 9-year-old.

From the living room window, Velma could see her boys playing football on the vacant lot across the street. She knew the other boys were Raymond's age, but little John David managed to hold his own. Now, however, word had come that he had followed Raymond down to the high school field after school, and he was begging the coach for a uniform, reasoning his participation would give that year's varsity an extra scrub to scrimmage against.

Velma put her foot down.

"I can't stand the thought of you getting hurt," she said, trying to soothe John David's frustration. "We can't afford any broken bones around here anyway."

But in time she came to realize John David did not merely enjoy playing athletics; his need bordered on fanatical. A zeal like his would not likely be dampened by a mother's tears.

And so, just as Harry had done for Raymond, Velma backed off, and John David was issued football equipment for the first time in the seventh grade.

There, along with the eighth and ninth graders, he played for the B-team, the daily practice victims for Raymond's varsity squad. On the day uniforms were handed out, little John David sat outside with the other boys and waited for his name to be called. The coach kept motioning others into the locker room, until only a few remained.

"Ya'll come on in and pick from what's left," the coach said.

John David found an old scuffed-up helmet, some pads that smelled like week-old potato salad, and a pair of shoes so big and roomy it really didn't matter both were left-footed.

Fully dressed, he went out and began his duties as a blocking dummy.

By the start of his sophomore season with the Springhill Lumberjacks, John David weighed in at a most respectable 165 pounds. Less than four months later, as the season drew to a close, he topped out at a hearty 185.

John David shrugged off the growth as one of those sudden spurts that can happen to anybody, while asking for second helpings. Harry Crow snorted, "You can thank Dr. Garrett. I told him to give me some pills that would make me gain weight, and sure enough you did."

Springhill was a town of 2,500 mostly family-oriented citizens living peacefully amid the 70-foot high pines, huge oaks and an occasional gravel pit. There was no town square, no stoplights. Main Street was a two-lane blacktop, its storefronts stretching less than a half-mile.

Almost every dad in the surrounding vicinity worked at the paper mill, where they mostly turned pulpwood into brown-paper, corrugated boxes. Some fathers, like Harry, were also members of the Springhill Booster Club (like the other dads, ol' Harry had become quite a football expert after observing a few of his boys' games).

Velma tended the cash register at the General Mercantile store – a clothing, hardware and grocery outlet all rolled into one. But she always had time for the First Methodist Church, and she saw to it that her children looked prim and proper as they attended services each and every Sunday morning and evening.

Nobody in Springhill had air-conditioning, and television was still over the next horizon. But the Crows' attic fan in the hallway sucked in enough cool air, their little ice box kept food and beverages fresh, and the cow out back furnished all the buttermilk a family of six could want. Plus, they could tune in The Louisiana Hayride on the radio, live from Shreveport, less than an hour away.

People in Springhill did not fuss over conditions. If anybody was poor, nobody talked about it because everybody in town pretty much lived like everybody else. Absolutely no one had yet come up with a good reason why a door should be locked; having to search for the keys and unlock it again was just a nuisance.

For years, John David has been fond of saying, "Springhill is so far back in the woods, they have to pipe in sunshine." But he was no Huckleberry Finn trampling around in the nearby thicket. He did not spend his spare time whispering back at the pines, or popping doves from tree branches with a BB gun. Only occasionally was he seen with a fishing pole or rifle in his hands.

John David's parents, Harry and Velma, prior to their first airplane trip en route to New York City for the Heisman dinner in 1957.

John David's heart always carried him, magnet-like, toward the vacant lots and outside basketball courts.

Other boys did not go to those lots and dirt courts to tease John about the odd expression frozen on his face. They, too, went to play ball. But they did tease, cruelly and often.

When John David was in grade school, Raymond and his sisters were quick to silence the derogatory comments about "Crook Face," and the meanness behind the question, "How come you always grinnin'?" Nobody in the family ever fussed over John David's face or made a big to-do over it, so why should anyone else?

John David grew old enough to defend himself and fought back with his fists, again and again, but he nev-

er did completely silence the taunts. The fighting went on until one day the other boys simply grew accustomed to his face.

In the 20 years the Crow family lived in Springhill, few people moved in or out. Every face in town became a familiar one sooner or later, which is probably a good thing for everyone since John David was not inclined to close himself up in his room.

At 10, he built a shoeshine box and walked the streets of Springhill looking for customers. When the box caved in, he nailed together another one and hit the streets again. Neighbors paid him to mow their lawns and to bring them buttermilk from the cow.

John David knew he looked different. The mirror didn't lie. But nothing could be done about it. It's not like he was the Hunchback of Notre Dame, so why feel ashamed?

John David's confidence grew best on any playing field. Prior to his sophomore year at Springhill High, he was paid a high compliment by Coach Billy Baucum. Normally the cautious sort when it came to praising individual Lumberjacks, when Coach Baucum informed a few good folks at Tennyson's Drugstore that John David had a chance to be a good one because he had *heart*, he flamed the town with the kind of gossip that can cause the fall air to crackle.

A few years back, Raymond's junior year, Springhill won the Class A Northern Louisiana championship. Now, something special just might be on its way again, and wouldn't that be something?

John David knew he could run with a football, and when he squared up and stuck his helmet into a ball carrier, the one who ended up on his back never seemed to be him. He had heard some of the talk and knew it was going around town. And the girls, he sensed, were beginning to regard him as something of a "big man on campus." He had a sharp, blond crewcut, a decent build and deep blue eyes.

Why not live up to this suddenly appealing reputation?

John David had marveled at John Wayne on the big screen and had seen almost every movie the Duke had made. John David did not envision becoming a movie star, but if everybody was going to treat him like John

"We haven't even met ... Where I come from, people don't just start talking to somebody they don't even know – much less ask them out on a date."

Carolyn Gilliam

Wayne for awhile, what was it gonna hurt?

Besides, maybe Coach Baucum knew what he was talking about.

John David never intended to be cocky in a loud, brash way. For one thing, his father wouldn't allow it. Just that summer, John David had sassed his mother in the kitchen one evening, and Harry Crow, who had paddled but not laid a hand on any of his children, cuffed John David across the face, hard, with an open paw. John staggered backward several steps and when he looked at his dad again, the hand was doubled in a fist.

"Next time," Harry growled, incensed, "it's going to be closed."

John David avoided his father's fists, and in the meantime ran into a rare new girl in town, Carolyn Gilliam. They met between classes in the hallway the first day of their sophomore year.

Rumor had it she'd just moved down from Sparkman, Arkansas, a saw mill town, to live with her brother and his wife. She was 15 years old and more radiant than the big July 4th firecracker celebration as she walked through the halls that morning, causing shy boys nearby to stir slowly and form small, imaginary circles on the floor with their shoes, while the girls checked their lipstick.

John David pulled his head out of the clouds and swaggered right up to the new girl.

"I sure would like to take you out on a date."

Carolyn flinched, a deer exposed by oncoming headlights. She did not want to cause a scene her first day at Springhill High. She had met a few of the school's 200 or so students, but only in passing, whereas every one of them knew all they cared to know about each other.

"We haven't even met," she replied, hoping her voice would not carry down the hallway.

John David looked dumbfounded as she bravely continued, "Where I come from, people don't just start talking to somebody they don't even know – much less ask them out on a date."

John David walked off, never intending to ask again. He didn't, for 2½ years, though he did see Carolyn around campus and town, and they did become friendly.

They usually smiled and chatted briefly when they ran into each other down at Tennyson's, the corner drugstore where everybody convened at the soda fountains; and at the Dothel House, Springhill's variation of the small-town Dairy Queen, though sometimes she was there with John David's sister, Yvonne, or one of his Lumberjack teammates.

He'd spot her at the drive-in movie theater, he in a jalopy full of guys, she among the girls in the car a few rows up. Those nights, high-schoolers borrowed the keys to daddy's

Carolyn Gilliam — the prettiest girl in Springhill, La.

ing aid since he was 14, when he first began to lose most of his hearing, but it didn't stop Johnnie Ray from becoming one of the great jukebox kings of the early 1950's.

Perhaps just as her girlfriends could not turn away from Ray's mournful cries, Carolyn Gilliam over time could no longer deny her interest in John David Crow, or J.D., as some knew him.

Only his mother called him John David – until he began dating Carolyn the winter of their senior year. Carolyn recognized a maturity in John David not obvious in other boys. He seemed to want to amount to something extra.

When she heard Velma refer to him as "John David" so casually around the house, Carolyn liked the sound. A name like John David had more substance, and a more mature ring to it than J.D., or even John.

So John David it was, for the two women now in his life.

Less than two years later, a legendary, Bunyanesque American icon named Paul (Bear) Bryant took to calling him John David, too. Over a 38-year career that included six national championships, Bryant almost always referred to players by last name or jersey number – except John David.

Only when Bear started using both names did everyone else follow, and soon John Crow was being called John David by people who would never even meet him; and, young farm boys all over the belly of Central Texas were named John David, after him, in the late 1950's and early 60's.

But all of that would come later.

This was still six months before Carolyn and John David would graduate – before the prettiest little thing in high school and the hardest-working Lumberjack going, the one with the peculiar facial paralysis, would shock and bewilder family members and friends by marrying and moving ridiculously far away, to some little place in Texas called College Station.

car and clogged traffic on both sides of Main (they called it "dragging Main.") John and Carolyn might notice each other in separate cars and nod.

Though neither spent much time on the dance floor, they did say "hi" at the city swimming pool, where on summer nights teenagers jitter-bugged and waltzed and stuffed nickels into the jukebox to hear *Cry* and *The Little White Cloud That Cried*, both by the amazing Johnnie Ray.

Nicknamed "The Prince of Wails" by his adoring throngs, most of them female, Johnnie Ray wore a large, noticeable hearing aid in one ear. He had worn a hear-

CHAPTER TWO

The Pride of Springhill, La.

Nobody wondered much whether John Crow would ever be great enough to win the Heisman Trophy or play pro ball, mainly because people in Springhill were not inclined to daydream that way.

Oh, John could run with a pigskin, and his heroics pumped a life into that blue-collar, callused-hands town like nothing before or since, except maybe the paper mill. But every town in the parish and state had a football hero.

Why, just that year there was a big kid down in South Louisiana, name of Jim Taylor, who ran over people just like their John David did. Still others in Shreveport, Monroe, Alexandria, on down around Lake Charles and points in between, were talented enough to cause old-timers perched in the stands to draw on their pipes and shake their heads slowly, sideways, in awe.

But they would be doing it again next year, too, for somebody else.

High school football made for a splendid autumn diversion. It had a way of causing folks of all ages to congregate on a few rows of wooden benches – kinda like church, except outdoors, and with all the denominations present, pulling together.

Every Saturday morning following Friday night games, that year's Springhill varsity sat around on the curb out-

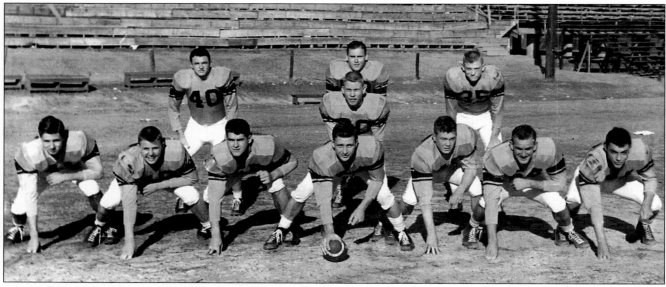

Springhill High won the Louisiana Class A State Championship in 1952.

side Tennyson's Drugs and rehashed the latest tussle. Passers-by joined in, getting an injury update and offering praise or condolences, whichever was appropriate. The tradition had been going on for many years before the Crows arrived in Springhill and has continued the many years since.

But that's all it was – a high school game. The lucky ones got to play two or three years, and come graduation even they had to think about what they were really going to do with their lives.

Of course, if you could get your hands on one of those rare college scholarships ... well now, that was a whole 'nuther story. Those college grants didn't grow on trees, but if you played football it didn't hurt your chances.

One day Raymond's senior year, a coach from Louisiana Tech dropped in. Raymond had drawn some attention as a 185-pound lineman. When the recruiter suggested a four-year scholarship might be in the offing, every ear at the table perked up, including John David's. None of the Crows had considered college a remote possibility until then.

Velma and Harry wanted their four children to enjoy the best education possible, but they never discussed paying anybody's way to college. They could have kept their early savings in a cigar box. They weren't poor, but they had spent years digging out from under the Depression,

sometimes with a small shovel. Just when they figured finances were leveling out, another baby came along.

In the seventh and eighth grades, John David helped by sacking groceries at the General Mercantile; and, he paid for his school clothes by working for the City of Springhill from the eighth through the 10th grades, cutting grass, pulling weeds, pouring more chlorine into the swimming pool. Even after practices and day games as a junior and senior, he worked one odd job or another.

Sure enough, Raymond did accept that scholarship and left home. Not too much later, Doris married and moved across town. With only two kids left in the Crow household, life seemed like a steal.

One day in the spring of John David's senior year, Harry climbed a nearby telephone pole and stuck an antenna on top. The antenna was not much competition for the tall pines, but the Crows had their first television set. It picked up one station, in Texarkana, which came in pretty well most of the time.

Of course, the whole country was pumped up and still feeling its oats in the afterglow of World War II. All you had to do was head down to the Pines Drive-In or the indoor movie theater on Main and watch John Wayne in *The Sands of Iwo Jima* or Gregory Peck in *Twelve O'Clock High* to know the kind of heart Americans had in 'em after whipping Hitler and Japan.

If you got there early enough or sat through a feature, you could even catch the latest Movietone News reel.

In *Twelve O'Clock High*, a few American bombers are stuck in England, whining and feeling sorry for themselves, when their newly arrived commander, General Savage (that would be Gregory Peck), storms into a briefing and spits out disgustedly: "Consider yourselves already dead." Well, that was like having ice water thrown in their faces. Pride aroused, those boys rushed out and made something of themselves.

And Shane? Why, a movie never better defined the times. Alan Ladd was as wholesome and righteous as a vanilla shake – the kind of boy who would have enjoyed growing up in Springhill. Jack Palance dressed in black, drank black coffee from a blackened pot, and scared children and small dogs while leering at the wives.

Everybody at the drive-in and everybody in the theater rooted for the same side. It was just that way at football games. Our boys against yours.

Who needed dreams about tomorrow? John David loved a game called football and a girl named Carolyn, and he enjoyed a steady diet of each. He could not imagine life getting any better.

Of course, if he wanted to dream, he could tune into the LSU and Tulane games on the radio. In junior high, he could pick up the Southern Methodist University games from Dallas' Cotton Bowl, where Doak Walker ran with such abandon they had to build another tier to the stadium. Football, especially that played in college and high school, was prospering right along with everything else.

Springhill won the Louisiana Class A championship in football in 1952, when John David was a junior. The one-time scrawny boy had grown all right, to 6-2, 195 pounds, and was still growing. His battering runs were too much for most tacklers to handle. Some of them got hurt, and some of them just didn't want to have to tackle him again.

On game day, store owners up and down Main hung out their "CLOSED" signs and, underneath, scribbled such things as, "WE'VE GONE TO THE GAME! WHY HAVEN'T YOU?"

Most everyone did. People came out of the sur-rounding pines in their pickups and curious fans came as far away as Shreveport to watch the Lumberjacks play. Some Friday nights, attendance at the modest high school field doubled the town's population. Reserved seating seemed a might silly and pompous, but businessmen who had to work late, like A.C. Higginbotham, always had a friend save a spot by throwing a blanket on one of the wooden benches.

The most legendary game that junior season did not occur in the playoffs or even in district competition. Byrd High was one of the two biggest schools in Shreveport, when Class AA was the largest classification in the state. Byrd's principal and coach had offered Springhill $500 to come on down. Headlines in the Shreveport daily newspaper suggested everyone turn out "to welcome these country boys to town for a scrimmage."

A record 20,000 showed up at Fairgrounds Stadium that day, and they saw a lot of Byrd boys grasp at thin air when they weren't already on their backs.

Billy Baucum's strategy was fairly basic. Give the ball to John David and watch him go. Crow and backfield star Virgil Jester had gotten proficient at pitching laterals to each other just before being tackled, and their savvy unnerved the Byrd boys.

Hal Morehead, who played end for Byrd, later recounted, "That scoundrel Crow would be coming at you, and you never knew whether he'd run, or pass, or what."

Springhill embarrassed Byrd, 34-7.

By John David's senior year, he was 6-2, 200. Few defensive linemen were anywhere near as big; few backs as fast.

Byrd still wanted a piece of him. Late in the season, the Lumberjacks again took a bus down to Shreveport to play an extremely fired-up Byrd varsity.

Another record crowd, this one 22,000 strong, turned up, many hungering for revenge.

Byrd was undefeated, Springhill 8-1. A separated shoulder had caused John David to miss the opener, which Springhill lost, 13-7. But the Lumberjacks averaged 46 points a game for eight consecutive victories — seven times breaking 40.

This time, Byrd muscled "the country boys" early and put them in a 20-6 hole that looked to get a whole lot deeper.

That's when Billy Baucum switched to a double-wing, allowing the ball to be hiked directly to John David. Baucum reduced his offense to three plays: Crow off right tackle, Crow off left tackle, and Crow with the option to race around end or pass.

Back came Springhill, first on a long march culminated by a grinding touchdown by Crow and then, very late in the game, on a Crow touchdown pass to his buddy, Jack Montgomery. Springhill had pulled to within one, with the extra point to come.

There was no two-point conversion, and kicking the extra point was such an iffy thing that coaches could also choose to line up and run or pass for the point.

When Crow split the uprights, the Springhill contingent howled and celebrated the 20-20 comeback. But a motion penalty was called, causing Coach Baucum to stamp around on the sidelines as if someone had given him a hot-foot. Springhill fans booed and then quieted and watched the official step off the five-yard penalty.

Again, John David booted the ball through, and the 20-20 tie with the bigger, more talented Byrd squad tasted almost as sweet as victory for those making the 45-minute drive back deeper into the darkness.

Hopes of another state championship were thrashed, however, when district rival Minden upset the Lumberjacks, 27-12, in the season finale. Stunningly, the great Springhill team had failed to make the playoffs.

But the late-season disappointment did nothing to impede the number of college recruiters combing over Louisiana road maps, looking for a better way to get to Springhill.

Statistics at the time are sketchy, but John David easily averaged more than 100 yards a game, and in many games averaged more than 15 yards a carry. He scored 19 touchdowns and six extra points.

He had 40 pounds on many good college halfbacks, and before graduating from Springhill was clocked at 9.9 in the 100-yard dash – on an old cinder track, in shoes with long spikes.

Paul (Bear) Bryant was coaching his final season at Kentucky that fall of 1953. One day he stepped into a tar-black room and flipped on a projector and watched the sometimes choppy, black-and-white film of those Springhill-Byrd games.

Upon observing Crow for the first time, Bryant told an assistant coach, "That was a man playing amid a bunch of boys." Similar comments have been made about thousands of others since, but when Bear made his observation it was still fresh, if not completely original.

By then, nobody doubted that John David and a handful of Lumberjack teammates would be headed somewhere on football scholarships. That many boys from one senior class was certainly an accomplishment and spoke well for Billy Baucum's program.

According to the common consensus down at Tennyson's Drugs, the Dothel House, the pool hall, and other establishments along Main Street, no matter where this bunch of Lumberjacks decided to go, they were all scrappers who stood a fair chance of graduating with degrees, leading each to a fine job, whether it was in an office or not.

Carolyn knew John David would be leaving town after graduation. Some aspects of football might have seemed a bit complicated and technical as she watched games with the rest of the pep squad, but it didn't take a Bear Bryant to figure which Lumberjack was going to get the ball those downs the entire town sucked in its collective breath and prayed for the best.

As soon as Carolyn and John David started dating late that senior football season, they stopped going out with anyone else. But a month shy of graduation ceremonies, Carolyn's future was as up in the air as a tipped pass.

Her most realistic educational opportunity awaited at some business school, where she could learn to be a secretary. But her parents, who had moved to Springhill after she did, planned to move to Florida following her graduation. They really wanted her to go with them.

John David was certain enough of the inevitable he told his parents: "If they take her to Florida, I'm gonna go after her."

In most small towns, it seemed perfectly understandable that the girl chosen Most Beautiful in her class and the football hero would share at least a passing

John David — the hero of the 22-20 win over Byrd High of Shreveport — enjoys a well-deserved victory ride.

fancy for each other.

But Yvonne, the youngest Crow, overheard the surprised reactions of others when Carolyn began dating her brother. A sophomore cheerleader, Yvonne was good friends with Carolyn and often went on double-dates with them.

The whispering around them was not enough to keep John David and Carolyn from dating throughout basketball season, when he jumped center and played forward and led Springhill to the 1953-54 state title. The Lumberjacks beat Minden five times that season, including the state finals in Lafayette, helping ease the pain of the football defeat.

With the end of their high school days fast approaching, John David decided to go for broke. The thought of Carolyn living a thousand miles away was more than he could stomach. He asked her to marry him, and to go off to college with him.

He was 18, she was 17, and once they made their decision they never looked back.

In those days of unlimited college visitations, many recruiters appeared at the Crow household in the spring of 1954. They came from Arkansas, Baylor, LSU, Mississippi, Mississippi State, Oklahoma, Rice, SMU, TCU, Texas, Texas A&M, Tulane and most other college football powers in the 1950's.

These recruiters had seen far too many college careers wilt away in a woman's arms, and they advised John David the smartest thing a young man could do in his situation was attend college on his own (there'd be a mess of pretty ones waiting on campus).

But when John David informed them he most definitely would be marrying Carolyn Gilliam, and she most definitely would be accompanying him, they began phoning and visiting her house, too.

Of all the college recruiters, Elmer Smith proved to be the most important, and, soon, one of the most pivotal people in John David's life.

Raymond Crow's scholarship at Louisiana Tech had been short-lived. He walked off campus early, the day the varsity put the freshmen through their annual haz-

John David also starred for the Springhill basketball team.

ing. Raymond thought the whole ordeal ridiculous and instead went to work rough-necking in the oil fields. Then he married without telling his dad, and took a job at the paper company. Shortly thereafter, Raymond decided college didn't seem like such a bad idea after all, and he jumped at a junior college scholarship to Magnolia A&M, in southwest Arkansas but only 30 miles from Springhill. The coach there was Elmer Smith.

During that time, the college was upgraded to a four-year university and renamed Southern State. Harry and John David drove to every home game. Coach Elmer (as the Crows called him) even let them stand on the sidelines.

By John David's senior season, Coach Elmer was resigned to the fact that the boy was just too good for his small-college program.

When John David visited officially, Coach Elmer sat him down in his office and said, "I know you can play this game on a higher level, and I'm not about to hold you back. But do me a favor and meet a couple of our alums, who are waiting down the hall. Just let them make their pitch, nod your head a few times, and then you can go."

Meanwhile, Bear Bryant was growing weary at Kentucky, where Adolph Rupp, the basketball coach, hogged all the headlines. And not all of them were good. Kentucky's basketball program had just completed a year without playing basketball due to NCAA ban for a variety of recruiting violations, and their boosters rallied energetically around Rupp.

Bear Bryant did not play second fiddle. At the close of the 1953 season, his eighth at Kentucky, he simply resigned, mysteriously and surprisingly to many, without a job. But one was open at Texas A&M, whose Aggies had beaten Bear's Wildcats in the season opener before Kentucky pieced together a 7-2-1 record. Bear had admired the spirit of the Cadets in the stands that day.

Southwest Conference head coaching positions were typically filled by staff assistants or high school coaches. Bear's hiring sent a ripple through Texas and Arkansas.

One of the first assistant coaches Bear hired was Coach Elmer, whose first and perhaps only assignment during the entire spring of 1954 was to reside on the doorsteps of the Crow household.

Coach Elmer phoned John David immediately and said, "John, I've just been hired by Texas A&M. Now I'm at that next level, and I wanna get you to come here."

For three months, Coach Elmer stayed at a small hotel near Springhill and spent more morning time on the Crow sidewalk than a daily newspaper. Years later, Elmer admitted, "John David got so disgusted with me hanging around so much he said, 'Coach, I don't know whether I'll be able to finish high school or not.' "

Coach Elmer knew that nothing in recruiting was a lock. John visited several universities. He made his first train ride, out of Shreveport all the way down Louisiana to the Louisiana State campus in Baton Rouge. He liked LSU's coach, Gus Tinsley, but, a couple of LSU alumni, even closer to the Crow family than they were to their beloved alma mater, got wind of an upcoming coaching change.

When the two alumni cautioned Harry, LSU lost out.

One day, John David and his buddy, Virgil Jester, were picked up by the biggest, blackest Lincoln Continental either of them had ever seen. An oil man from Oklahoma, and a serious Sooner booster, drove them to his house in Ardmore. The house was bigger than downtown Springhill. John and Virgil ate an impressive dinner in a huge dining room and slept in a bedroom bigger than either of their homes. The bedroom had an intercom, and it wasn't until years later that John David suspected the alumnus was probably listening in on their conversations that night.

Bud Wilkinson's flashy Sooners played their annual spring game the next day, a game that pitted former players against the coming season's varsity. John and Virgil were amazed to find roughly 100 football players suited in the same stadium, which also, by the way, was quite huge.

But it was one of the littlest guys in a helmet, Tommy McDonald, who ran amok, dashing around end, darting inside tackles on such effortless romps the defensive line looked helpless and groggy. McDonald put on a display that not only thrilled Sooner backers but caused John David on the sidelines to mutter to Virgil, "I'll never get to play here."

A few weeks later, John David, his parents, and fel-

They talked about football, what it meant to the coach, and what winning meant to the coach. And finally Bear Bryant said, "If you want to play a lot and win a lot, come to A&M. You'll get that chance."

low Lumberjack Jack Montgomery visited Texas A&M in College Station, as far away from Springhill as LSU or Oklahoma. Coach Elmer took them to the Aggies' spring game, and John David saw a varsity so thin that players were swapping jerseys with each other in order to play different positions.

The Aggies had the typical three-yards-and-a-cloud-of-dust offensive mentality. Nobody ran like Tommy Mc-Donald.

John David said to Coach Elmer, "Gosh, I probably can play here pretty quick."

Coach Elmer said, "Son, I'm not going to lie to you. I know what you can do. You could play here an awful lot as a sophomore."

Since freshmen could not compete on the varsity, those words made a powerful impression on John David. When they returned to Springhill, John David told Carolyn about Texas A&M.

Velma had tired of recruiters by then. She informed her boy: "All these people don't need to be spending all their money coming to visit us. If you'd sign a few letters, the others could use their money more wisely."

There was no national signing date at the time, only different conference letters of intent. John David signed a Southeast Conference letter with LSU and a Big Eight letter with Oklahoma.

Before Coach Elmer helped him decide on Texas A&M, John David had been most impressed by Rice University among the Southwest Conference schools. Coach Baucum had taken his squad to Dallas on a school bus for the 1954 Cotton Bowl Classic. John and his teammates sat in the end zone that day and watched Rice's Dicky Maegle average 24.1 yards a carry and set a bowl record by rushing for 265 yards.

Maegle scored three touchdowns and Rice won, 28-6. From the stands, John David was peering directly down the Alabama sidelines when one of the most stunning plays in college football history occurred. Phantom tackler Tommy Lewis jumped off the Alabama bench to blindside Maegle, who was well en route to what was ruled a 95-yard touchdown run. John David also jumped up, but from the end zone seats, and yelled out, "What in the world is going on!"

Maegle's runs made Rice attractive to John David, who also liked Rice coach Jess Neely on his visit to Houston.

But his first trip to A&M clinched John David's decision. He could no more stomach the thought of sitting on a bench and watching others play football than he could of Carolyn moving away.

Still unsigned in the SWC, John David made one more visit to College Station and this time met alone with his future head coach, Bear Bryant. Coach Elmer had said,

John David and Carolyn were married in the summer of 1954 — prior to departing for Texas A&M.

"He just wants to sit with you for awhile, just you and him, over at the coffee shop in the student center."

Bear was living out of a suitcase at the Memorial Student Center, his family still back in Kentucky where his wife prepared for the move and their children completed the school term.

When John David walked into the coffee shop at 9 a.m., he eyed a large man sipping coffee and reading the papers. Bear Bryant's dark hair was messed, and he had on a pair of khakis, a pajama shirt, and house slippers.

John David looked beyond the garb and uncombed hair and thought, "This may be the most amazing man I have ever seen."

Bryant's presence was huge. He was physically bigger than John David and looked fierce. John David figured him capable of kicking any man's ass, but Bryant's eyes softened and brows narrowed kindly when he spoke.

They talked about football, what it meant to the coach, and what winning meant to the coach. And finally Bear Bryant said, "If you want to play a lot and win a lot, come to A&M. You'll get that chance."

And to make sure John David got that chance, Bryant out-foxed the other SWC coaches on the conference's signing day.

League rules dictated that all SWC letters of intent had to remain on college campuses until 8 a.m. signing day, at which time coaches dispersed in all directions. That gave schools closer to Springhill (SMU, TCU, Baylor) an edge over the Aggies.

With the help of some big Aggie backers in Shreveport who worked for United Gas, Bryant had John David's letter flown from the little airport in nearby Bryan to Shreveport in a private plane. Coach Elmer drove down that morning, grabbed the letter, returned to Springhill, and had John David's signature an hour before anyone else arrived.

Other coaches were astonished. Until then, none of them had considered flying a letter of intent to a prospect.

On July 2, 1954, Carolyn and John David Crow were married in the home of Springhill's First Methodist Church preacher. Yvonne served as maid of honor, and Billy Burns, a longtime friend, was best man. Family and a few close friends attended, but Carolyn and John David felt certain that almost everybody in town never thought they would last.

First of all, she is just too young. And how do they expect to pay bills when all that boy is gonna be doing is attending college and playing football? You watch – one or both of 'em will be back before Thanksgiving.

The day Carolyn and John David tossed their meager belongings into the backseat and pointed their car toward Texas, a world of mystery stretched out ahead of them like some long highway, rolling over high and lowlands, taking them much farther than they could have possibly anticipated, perhaps as far as their minds could imagine.

CHAPTER THREE

Playing for the 'Bear'

Paul Bryant had been a head coach for nine football seasons and still was a week or two shy of turning 41 the day the teenage newlyweds, John David and Carolyn Crow, joined him in College Station.

The Crows pulled up to the College View Apartments one screaming-hot August afternoon in 1954, and looked around at the college view, and Carolyn's heart slid to the floorboard.

Her typical surroundings, green pines and running streams, had been replaced by brown. Flat brown earth, paper-sack brown buildings, brown-toned uniforms on all-male, leather-necked cadets.

Had she and John David strolled a mere mile south or east, they would have found themselves in a prairie. A very hot prairie. Egypt could not have been any more foreign.

And that was just outside.

The College View Apartments consisted of old veterans' barracks, each converted into eight to 12 apartments, none air-conditioned, most with two bedrooms to cater to families.

Velma and Harry had packed a little eight-inch cooling fan as a going-away present, but its soft, whirring blades were up against some stiff odds. Central and West Texas were frying, immersed in a mean seven-year drought. Even at night, temperatures stayed in the 90's.

Humidity turned starched shirts into drippy rags, and the steam bath bullied its way indoors, too.

Married student-athletes on scholarship lived in the renovated barracks, along with a great many veterans from the Korean War and World War II – most of them older and with their families, attending college on the GI bill.

A teenage couple fresh from sleeping in their own respective bedrooms would find life in College View a bit unfamiliar at times. But much of it would also be extremely exciting, the way things are for teenagers left to fend for themselves.

Paul Bryant had arrived that spring, knowing only a little more than Carolyn about College Station and Texas A&M. Bear's '53 Kentucky squad fell to the Aggies, 7-6, at Kyle Field only a few months before he switched allegiances, but he hadn't spent time wandering around campus. The only grass under Bryant's feet was that on the football field.

Even when A&M hired him, Bryant never went through a formal interview process on campus. He did not have to glad-hand to get the job – and he never did thereafter.

Bear's reputation was already growing, but little of his legend could be spotted in his rear-view mirror.

That spring of '54, while John David was finishing high school and sorting through all the college offers, Bryant was greeted by thousands of Cadets on arrival at Easterwood Airport.

That evening, the Cadets escorted their new leader to the Grove outdoor theater, site of the tradition-rich "12th Man" yell sessions. Almost 5,000 showed up, all in uniform, their cavalry boots spit-shined, the bottom halves of their ties neatly tucked inside the second and third buttons of their pressed shirts.

Virtually the entire student body attended; one would have had to be bed-ridden to miss it.

Bear squinted out from a stage only a few feet higher than the cadets standing in front. Others bunched around each side of the platform, the mob so large it bled far into the darkness.

Bryant flung off his sports coat and stomped on it, and the Aggies went nuts.

Then he unraveled his tie and stomped on it. And the Aggies went nuts some more.

He rolled his long-sleeve shirt above his elbows and grabbed the microphone with both hands, like Johnnie Ray tantalizing a thousand screaming girls, and proceeded to explain how he had come there to win. Nothing less would be permissible. The sea of Aggies roared, his words sweet music to their ears, and nourishment for sagging spirits.

Bear wasn't just spewing hot air. Legend has it, he phoned a half-dozen prominent Aggie alumni, all successful businessmen living in places like Dallas, Houston, Fort Worth and San Antonio, beckoning them to a private meeting on campus.

"If you can't make it, send your No. 1 lieutenant because we don't have time to waste," Bear said, or words to that effect.

The men were seated around a table when Bryant walked in. They waited anxiously as Bear, 6-4 and forever looming larger, shuffled over to the windows and, while looking out, tapped an unfiltered Chesterfield cigarette free of the pack, snapped open a lighter and puffed.

Then he exhaled and, as the story goes, turned and asked, "Gentlemen, how badly do you want a national championship?"

He went around the table one at a time, telling what each could do to help A&M athletics. A week later, the alumni returned with $20,000 to $25,000 apiece, and that's how Bear started his football program. Not everything in College Station was brown after all.

Hardly anyone knew Paul Bryant when Maryland gave him his first head coaching job in 1945.

The Terps were a broken-down jalopy of a program that appealed to only a few in the coaching profession. World War II had taken so many good young men from all playing fields that baseball's Detroit Tigers won the world championship that year with a starting lineup averaging 35 years in age. College football felt the dramatic impact just as severely.

But the era could not have been more perfect for Bryant. He loved the attitude of the soldiers home from the seas. The American soldier's dedication in the trenches spilled over into the locker room, and a number of war veterans helped Bryant's only Maryland team win

John David, Carolyn and their son, Johnny, at their apartment in College Station.

its last three games to finish 6-2-1.

Then, just like that, Bear was gone. He had kicked a tackle off the team for trying to drink up all the beer in Washington, D.C., one night. When Bryant returned from the Christmas holidays, he discovered the player had been reinstated by an assistant coach.

"I thought you were too hard on him so I let him back on," the assistant explained.

Bear wished him a happy future while drop-kicking his butt through a door; but Curly Byrd, an influential figure in D.C. and Maryland's president, sided with the assistant and the player. Bear resigned, and still in shock,

walked to his office, grabbed a few Western Union telegrams from his desk, and drove home.

One telegram happened to be from the University of Kentucky chancellor. Something about phoning collect if interested in the Wildcats' head coaching vacancy.

Bryant brought in a few good Marines, literally, and built the Wildcats into a national power. Kentucky enjoyed eight winning seasons, including Bryant's first flirtation with perfection in 1950. That's when Bryant's gritty bunch reeled off 10 victories in a row before falling to Tennessee, 7-0, in the regular season finale. The Wildcats finished 11-1 by beating Oklahoma in the Sugar Bowl.

The 1954 Aggie squad, which lost nearly half of the team at Junction, won only one game that season.

By then, Bryant had a reputation as a master psychologist, someone who never stopped listening or learning from other coaches around the country. He took what you did and did it better, often because he could will his boys to reach a higher level.

Bum Phillips, one of his assistants at A&M before establishing his own kind of legend with the Houston Oilers, was fond of saying, "Bear Bryant didn't coach football; he coached people."

When Bryant was hired at A&M, farmers everywhere could not have been more thrilled. Here was a man with spunk and spirit, coming to a school chock full of the stuff.

But the Aggies did not hire Bryant to start a football tradition; they hired him to propel A&M back to the good old days of Jarrin' John Kimbrough, and before.

In the immediate years leading up to Bear's arrival, Cadets had stood fidgeting through too many losses, including a ghastly stretch in 1948-49 when their team went 1-17-2. Alumni were weary of having to hearken all the way back to 1941 to cite a Southwest Conference crown, and to '39 to relive their national championship days.

John Kimbrough, a 210-pound fullback, was the runaway locomotive behind a 19-game winning streak and that national championship season his junior year. Jarrin' John could roto-root through lines and occasionally skirt around end, surprising opponents with his speed, if not his nimbleness.

Older Aggies loved talking about Coach Homer Norton's 1939 bunch, which gave up only one touchdown and 18 points while going 10-0 in the regular season.

Now they had a new warrior, Bryant, to lead them back to the future.

Bear figured to dominate the SWC by out-recruiting, out-practicing, out-homeworking, and out-smarting everyone else.

But he never anticipated the difficulty of recruiting young, excitable boys to an all-male military college in a virtual outpost town.

Almost everyone who attended A&M was a white farm boy. A city slicker was someone from Wichita Falls or Temple. But these were the giddy post-war 50's, and many of the state's talented athletes, even the farm boys, preferred a landscape dotted with pink-cheeked lasses.

A&M's unflattering nickname, "Sing Sing on the Brazos," might not have seemed too far-fetched to Carolyn Crow the day she and John David arrived.

John David had not chosen Texas A&M for its landscape. Nor – rampant rumors to the contrary – did he go because A&M bought him. Fat-cat alumni from several college powerhouses had made some very appealing offers, not only to John David but to most of his talented freshman mates. A&M was no purer, and no more unethical, than most of the others.

A four-year scholarship sounded awesome enough; some of the offers caused John David's head to spin.

"Just before school starts, Coach Bryant is planning this special camp, somewhere way out in the woods, and nobody but football players and football coaches will be invited."

Elmer Smith

During recruiting visits, players swapped details of what they were being offered by various schools, drawing comparisons and perhaps stretching their tales a bit in the process.

But ultimately, John David's decision came down to a promise that Coach Elmer made to him just before signing day.

"Even if you get hurt and never play a down," Elmer said, "I'll see to it that you don't lose your scholarship."

So John David went to A&M to play football, and to earn a college degree – a feat not often accomplished by any Crow in family history.

John David had never played for anyone other than Billy Baucum, whose duties included basketball and track, as well as football. (John David did not even care for track and would have given it up had it not been for one of Baucum's firmest rules: no track, no football.)

But it was Harry Crow who really prepared his boy, and likely Carolyn, to deal with a man like Bear Bryant. Harry could not stand hanging around anyone, male or female, who did not work hard. His philosophy was as basic as meat-and-potatoes: Anything worth doing is worth doing right. Pats on the back were wholly unnecessary.

Paul Bryant would be no more prone to pats. Gentle ones, anyway.

John David and Carolyn showed up at A&M early, ten days before the start of the fall semester, because Coach Elmer had whispered a secret into his ear.

"Just before school starts," Elmer said, "Coach Bryant is planning this special camp, somewhere way out in the woods, and nobody but football players and football coaches will be invited."

John David was beside himself with excitement. In his life, he had attended one summer camp, sponsored by the First Methodist Church of Springhill. He could not imagine anything better than living out in the woods with his new teammates and concentrating on nothing but football.

When Coach Elmer dropped by the apartment to apologize and inform him that the camp did not include the freshmen, John David was heartbroken. He stood across the street from a dormitory one morning and watched two busloads of A&M's varsity depart for a place called Junction, Tex., 300 miles from campus.

Ten days later, one bus returned, half-loaded with 27 weary players.

Bryant took his scraggly bunch to Junction to avoid nosy alumni, who had watched nervously from the stands when he put his squad through rigid workouts on campus his first spring. Some 120 enthusiastic Aggies had reported for spring training. Their meager abilities appalled Bear. He cut or ran off all but about 80 – as the alumni looked on.

The whittling process grew even more earnest in Junction, a little-known town of 2,500 in the Hill Country. Texas A&M had purchased an old army base there called the Annex. Physics and geology majors used it earlier in the summer as a training facility. Bryant ordered a level area picked free of large rocks and cactus and marked it off as a field.

Practices began at 5 each morning before breakfast. Players napped until noon on cots inside screened-in, tin-roofed Quonset huts. Exhausted, players returned to the field later that afternoon, in pads still sticky from the morning workouts. The sun was only on a low broil then.

Many players fainted. Others suffered heat stroke. And most slipped away late at night, hitch-hiking home, as far away from Bear Bryant as they could get.

Bryant's hiring at A&M had caused quite a stir around the Southwest Conference, and writers on the annual pre-season press tour were curious to see what kind of outfit Bear was shaping up in Junction.

But only Mickey Herskowitz, a young, talented writer with The Houston Post, had any idea what was really going on there. He had been assigned to the Aggies full-time, and he saw firsthand how the players, their tongues dragging in the dust, feared their new coach.

"When he stood in the middle of the field," Herskowitz says in his 1983 book, *The Legend of Bear Bryant*, "the players walked around him as though he were a swamp."

The press tour came through after a day in Austin, where writers viewed the 100-plus players working out with the University of Texas. The scribes were flabbergasted by Bear's puny group.

Blackie Sherrod of The Fort Worth Press told Jones Ramsey, A&M's sports information director, he might as well forget about composing the typical three-deep player chart.

"You're the only SID in the country," Sherrod said, "who could type his roster sideways, double-spaced on a single sheet of 8-by-11 paper."

Those who survived have become famous in Aggie lore as "the Junction Boys." They formed a bond perhaps unlike any in college football history. Eight of them – gritty soldiers named Dennis Goehring, Lloyd Hale, Bobby Drake Keith, Bobby Lockett, Jack Pardee, Dee Powell, Gene Stallings, and Don Watson – won a Southwest Conference championship two years later.

The NCAA was less impressed, immediately passing a rule banning its colleges from practicing off campus thereafter.

Bear never batted an eye. He had a program to build. An example of the Junction gumption he wanted returning with him to College Station: One day he ordered his trainer, Smokey Harper, who had followed him from Kentucky, to run off a certain pudgy sophomore named Dennis Goehring, who didn't seem to have the necessary toughness. Bryant had been the first coach to promise Goehring a one-year scholarship. "All you gotta do," Bear said, "is still be on the team after fall practices."

Goehring was an 11th-string lineman when spring drills began, and he was still on the last team (seventh) when the buses headed for Junction.

Harper did as ordered and ridiculed the boy. But Goehring, who had watched a good many others on full scholarship walk away, never backed down, and one day finally spit back, "Smokey, I'll be hear long after you and Bryant are both gone."

Only 185 pounds, Goehring became an all-America guard as a senior and years later opened a bank in College Station. One of his first stockholders was Bear Bryant.

John David learned soon enough what he had missed out on by not being allowed to go to camp. Practices back on campus were no stroll in the park. The primary differences: you had a bed to sleep in instead of a cot; and the practice fields on campus were not strewn with thousands of those annoying, hidden burrs that pricked fallen players every down in Junction.

But the fear factor remained as great on campus. The fear of losing a scholarship, the fear of teammates knowing, the fear of giving up in front of Bear Bryant.

Pardee, a year ahead of John David, recalls, "The toughest thing is they never gave you any water back

PLAYING FOR THE 'BEAR'

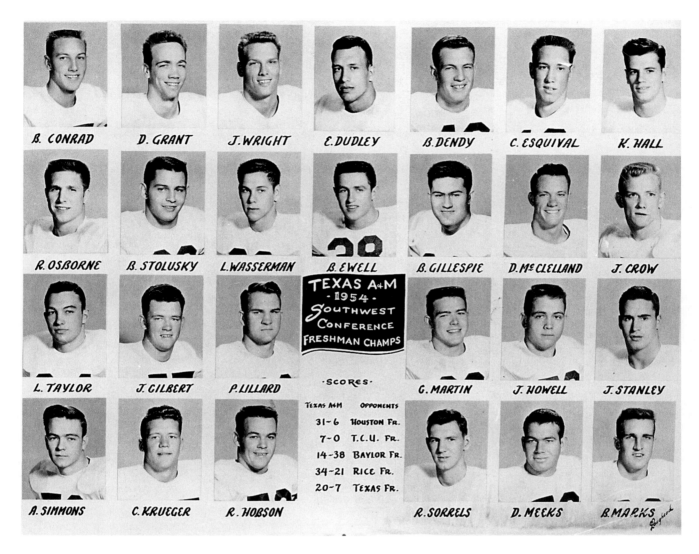

B. CONRAD   D. GRANT   J. WRIGHT   E. DUDLEY   B. DENDY   C. ESQUIVAL   K. HALL

R. OSBORNE   B. STOLUSKY   L. WASSERMAN   B. EWELL   B. GILLESPIE   D. McCLELLAND   J. CROW

L. TAYLOR   J. GILBERT   P. LILLARD   G. MARTIN   J. HOWELL   J. STANLEY

A. SIMMONS   C. KRUEGER   R. HOBSON   R. SORRELS   D. MEEKS   B. MARKS

TEXAS A&M
- 1954 -
SOUTHWEST
CONFERENCE
FRESHMAN CHAMPS

· SCORES ·

TEXAS A&M	OPPONENTS
31 - 6	HOUSTON FR.
7 - 0	T.C.U. FR.
14 - 38	BAYLOR FR.
34 - 21	RICE FR.
20 - 7	TEXAS FR.

then. Junction was a culture shock, but our practices back in College Station were probably hotter and more humid. We'd be on the field three to four hours in that heat, and lose 20 pounds in a day, but we were not allowed to drink water (during practice). That was rough."

The Junction survivors went 1-9 in Bear's first season, but he praised their desire and repeatedly said they laid the foundation for the SWC championship the Aggies would win two years later.

In 1954, most of the talent – and bodies — could be found in Bear's freshman crop, labeled "The Team of Tomorrow" by anxious Aggies. Bryant's recruiters thoroughly blitzed the state his first spring at A&M, taking advantage of the unlimited freshman rule to sign more

than 100 of them. Another 50 or so walked on.

Jerry Wizig, now a sportswriter for The Houston Chronicle, covered the first freshman game that year for the Aggie student paper.

"Everybody was looking forward to seeing these guys play for the first time," Wizig says. "What I remember most is sitting high up in the pressbox, watching them running out of the locker room. They just kept coming and coming. There were so many of them, some wore triple-digit numbers."

Of course, Bear ran most of them off, too.

Charlie Krueger, a 6-5 tackle from nearby Caldwell, says, "I really didn't like Bryant at all. My freshman year was a slow dance in a frying pan. He would do the

"The people who think we had it so easy weren't there. We seldom went out because we had to watch every dime we spent. My parents worried about us, and I was scared to death."

John David Crow

most unreasonable things to you, and then make you feel like a dog if you left."

Besides plucking John David out of Springhill, the Aggies signed another Louisiana talent, end Bobby Marks. Marks had originally checked into the dorms at LSU but slipped out that night and headed for College Station. (There are still reporters in Louisiana who believe John David was the one who sneaked off, but Crow's only stay at LSU came while participating in the state's North-South All-Star Game.)

The Texas load included prize running backs Bobby Joe Conrad and Jimmy Wright, as well as a virtual unknown, Roddy Osborne. Jim Stanley, a rugged guard, came out of Kentucky; Loyd Taylor, a fleet back from New Mexico, joined a startling stable of ball carriers.

None, not even John David, was as trumpeted as Kenneth Hall, the Sugar Land Express, perhaps the greatest high school football player of all time. Playing Class B ball, Hall in his senior year alone rushed for 4,045 yards and scored 57 touchdowns – despite sitting out the second halves of most games.

Against Houston Lutheran, he established a national single-game rushing record of 520 yards on only 11 car-

ries, a 47.3 average. The record was finally broken in 1974 by John Bunch of Elkins, Ark., who ran for 608 yards.

An asterisk is in order: Hall sat out the second half.

Bryant had been in attendance at an A&M booster club meeting in Houston when Hall was introduced to the roomful of men as the newest Aggie. Everyone stood and cheered mightily – for several minutes. When it came time for Bear to speak, he stood at the podium awhile, then drawled without a smile, "I'm damn happy to hear Kenneth Hall is coming to A&M. I hope he goes out for football."

Everyone busted a gut laughing, but Bear was not joking as much as they thought.

John David, now 6-2 and just over 200 pounds, remembers the first time he ever saw Kenneth Hall, who was a little bigger and a little faster, too.

"Just before the start of fall practices, the freshmen were told to report to the field one day," Crow says. "When I pulled up, I looked out at more than 100 people running around. One in particular stood out, and there was no doubt in my mind who it was. Ken Hall had these big legs. He was muscular and handsome. I remember it like yesterday.

PLAYING FOR THE 'BEAR'

"I looked down at my skinny, white legs and at my high-top shoes, went back to my car, and drove back to my apartment. I told Carolyn, 'I might have made a big, big mistake.' "

Hall was also sizing up Crow.

"I'd heard a little about him, so I was curious," Hall says. "From the first day, he carried himself with confidence. He was fair, honorable, and very tough – a statue of an individual."

They should have done great things together.

John David never stopped openly marveling at the fluidity of Hall's lightning runs. He knew he would never be that graceful.

Hall says, "If you just put a football in John's hands and watched him run, you'd go, "What's the big deal?'

"But he had a lean to his body when he ran, and a roll in his shoulders. Right when you were about to hit him, he'd lower his shoulder and absorb your blow, and you'd just slide off like a noodle. The next time, you'd be looking for the same thing, but he'd stick his helmet in there first and blow right over you.

"John was tough, and that's what Bryant wanted."

Because freshmen were not allowed to play on the varsity, the heroics of the "Team of Tomorrow" were performed in the shadows. They went 4-1 on an abbreviated freshman schedule, losing to Baylor. Bryant was so riled he worked them almost to death the next day.

John David rushed for 344 yards on 41 carries, an 8.3 average, and scored three touchdowns. He also intercepted three passes, punted three times for a 31.3 average, returned four kickoffs for 77 yards, and kicked two extra points. He and Jim Stanley were named to the Freshman All-SWC team.

Ken Hall led them in touchdowns, but he was having trouble adjusting to a system that forced him to play fullback on offense and inside linebacker on defense.

Bryant mostly used the talented freshmen to run scout-team plays during the week for the varsity. For a while, Bear allowed the freshmen to scrimmage the varsity, but they whipped the varsity so thoroughly that he halted the habit. Bad for morale, he said.

It would be another year before Bryant convinced college administrators to allow football players to skip Mil-

itary Science, a mandatory course including corps drills and marching practices.

Unlike their predecessors, John David and the other freshman football players (thanks to Bryant) did not have to march to chow. But they did attend Military Science when football was out of season (spring football, of course, was in season); and, in the famous Final Review, John David marched past the Commandant in the "B Athletics" Company.

On top of everything else, Carolyn announced she was pregnant: there would be another mouth to feed.

Through the years, Aggie lore has stretched reality completely out of whack concerning John David's lifestyle. There are those who believe he coasted through A&M, that teachers gave him grades and alumni were always there to toss another package of diapers into the shopping basket on its way past the cashier.

John David frowns and says, "The people who think we had it so easy weren't there. We seldom went out because we had to watch every dime we spent. My parents worried about us, and I was scared to death.

"Football was so tough. Finances were tough. Making decent grades was tough. Many times during my freshman year, I wasn't sure we were going to make it.

"Oh, Carolyn and I laughed a lot. We'd go to the drive-ins for a quarter and scrunch down in the front seat and hide while drinking a few beers. But we never dined out. We couldn't afford it. Usually, I'd eat lunch at the athletic dorm, and sometimes one of the cafeteria workers would slip me a plate of food to carry home to Carolyn."

Carolyn took a minimum-wage job at the campus bookstore, and it helped them scrape by, but there weren't enough hours in the day for all the practices, studying and corps obligations. The newlyweds saw each other every chance they could.

In June 1955, back in Springhill for the summer months before John David's sophomore year, Carolyn gave birth to a boy, named Johnny. John David and Carolyn had been married for only 11 months and already had withstood tough times.

Now, they would experience one of life's little miracles – a child. And they could only hope the next 11 months would be brighter.

CHAPTER FOUR

An Amazing Turnaround at A&M

Today's college football involves more good athletes and far superior conditioning, yet is dainty compared to the mud-in-your-eye game of the 1950's. Sort of like John Wayne and Pee Wee Herman both being actors, but ... a little different.

More often than not, the toughest Saturdays were relentless wrestling matches – especially if you played for Paul Bryant. And as rugged as the game was, even some of the football in the rough and tumble 50's seemed a might elegant through Bear's eyes.

The forward pass was a sissy's weapon to Bryant. He firmly believed passing softened the belly of a team worse than late-night carousing. He would rather rip off a toenail than score a quick touchdown.

Bear's logic: How do you expect to break the spirit of that same guy lining up across from you on every down, sometimes for the entire 60 minutes, if you don't begin the process right away?

Ultimate proof of Bryant's contempt for the easy score would come later, in John David's senior season, when quarterback Charlie Milstead drove the Aggies the length of the field against Missouri.

NCAA rules stipulated that the quarterback, not the coaches, call plays. Which means Milstead successfully (or so he thought) chose to toss a half-dozen crisp passes, leading the Aggies briskly down the field for a score on their first drive.

Bryant yanked Milstead before the extra point could be kicked, and when his confused quarterback returned to the sidelines Bear growled, "Don't ever do that again; you'll get them used to scoring easy touchdowns."

In John David's three varsity seasons under Bryant, James Wright put up the biggest passing numbers for an Aggie by completing 24 of 67 for 368 yards in 1955. Milstead led in '57, nailing 14 of 35 for 185 yards while sharing quarterbacking chores with Roddy Osborne.

To Bryant, the occasional pass was merely a change of pace, something to keep opponents off guard before the pounding began anew.

Nor did the Aggies amass phenomenal yardage on the ground under Bryant. Most teams of the era did not. A 100-yard rushing game then paralleled a 200-yard rushing day now.

As Charlie Krueger, the all-America tackle, puts it, "Bryant's offense was not designed around getting a runner in the open field so he could juke a tackler."

Oh, Jim Swink was jitterbugging around at TCU, doing his catch-me-if-you-can act most every Saturday in the fall. During John David's sophomore year in 1955, Swink became only the second player in Southwest Conference

Bryant's arrival at A&M stirred up the hopes of the Texas Aggie football faithful.

history to rush for more than 1,000 yards in a season. He reeled off 1,283 and led the nation with 20 touchdowns.

But there weren't many clever running schemes, no I-formation or Wishbone. There were a few run/pass options, but few of them involved split-second timing. Bryant employed the fashionable Split-T popularized by Bud Wilkinson's Oklahoma Sooners, but he liked watching his boys plow inside the tackles. He opted to eliminate risks and place the outcome on the fourth-quarter want-to and preparedness of his players.

Winning on the scoreboard was not enough. Bear's goal was to make certain everyone in the stands and everyone in both locker rooms knew which team owned the other. That meant physically and mentally beating down the guy across from you for three quarters, so that in the fourth you could whip him spiritually, too.

Dennis Goehring, the lineman Bryant failed to run off from Junction, says, "I can remember many times Coach Bryant telling us, 'The fourth quarter is when you win. It doesn't matter if it's the fourth quarter of this ballgame or the fourth quarter of life. When that ol' cotton gets in your throat, that's when you've got to keep going.' "

The most notable difference between the college game now and then was the one-platoon system with its limited number of substitutions. Lineups included only 11 starters, with every player going both ways, offensively and defensively, and someone among them handling kicking chores.

The one-platoon rule equally impacted

strategies and starting lineups. A starter could return once if subbed out of a particular quarter, but his back-up could not re-enter once removed. A manager would drape a shoestring around the player's neck to signify he was "dead" and, hence, could not return.

That's why Bryant's running backs did not carry the ball over and over and over. They had to conserve energy for defense – and there was no doubt in any player's mind which side of the ball mattered most to Bear.

They learned early that Bryant would never prefer a talented offensive player, such as Kenneth Hall at fullback and inside linebacker, over a superior defensive player at the same positions, such as Jack Pardee.

"It actually started with the Junction group, but by my sophomore year the trademarks of our team were gang-tackling and our willingness to hit hard," John David says. "We were taught that if you're on the field and standing up, you better be close to the ball carrier.

"I'm not saying Coach Bryant taught us to hit late; he despised penalties. But if a runner was still wiggling, you better have your hat on him."

John David was at safety in the spring training following his freshman year when he pulled up short after a tackle had been made ahead of him. The whistle blew, but John David was smacked from behind and knocked head-first into the pile.

He whirled around angrily to see who had applied the late hit, and noticed Bryant towering over him, pointing a very stiff finger into his face.

"Next time," Bear said in that gravelly voice, "you will get there before he's down."

The best football players were not the flashiest. They did everything well. A good running back could block, throw, catch, punt, return kicks, hit on defense and cover his area, perhaps convert an extra point or two, and – oh, yes – run and score touchdowns.

Individual statistics were something kept in baseball. In the 1950's, they were no measure of a football player. The game was all about winning and losing, and who was still standing.

And who was eligible to win championships and go to bowl games.

Probation, the result of recruiting violations, clouded

AN AMAZING TURNAROUND AT A&M

Elmer Smith oversees his linemen during practice in 1955. Bryant turned A&M from a SWC doormat to conference champions in only three seasons.

Bryant's stint at Texas A&M when possibly nothing else could have. At a conference meeting at Houston's Rice Hotel in the spring of 1955, the NCAA announcement came. Two years probation, covering John David's sophomore and junior seasons, including bowl games.

All the conventional staples apply. To wit: You do the crime, you pay the time.

But to the Aggies – whose players had a reasonably good idea what was going on at other programs, too – getting slapped for the reasons given was like having your driver's license revoked the first time you get caught doing 30 in a 20.

In *Bear*, his 1974 autobiography with John Underwood, Bryant admits:

"I know now we should have been put on probation. I know, too, I was not just trying to justify it in my mind when I said that if we were paying players, then other schools were doing it twice as bad, which some were. I'm not going to go soft on that point.

"I'm not sure how many of our boys got something; I guess about four or five did. I didn't know what they got, and I didn't want to know, but they got something because they had other offers and I told my alumni to meet the competition."

Someone in South Texas did. Two recruits signed affidavits saying they were promised $200 to sign and $50 a month over and above tuition.

The probation came the spring following the freshman season of Bear's "Team of Tomorrow," and casual assumption ever since, even among learned football fans, is that John David and others in his class committed the violations. The players' names, however, were Bob Manning and Tom Sestak.

"That probation had nothing to do with me or the class I was recruited in," John David says emphatically, some 40 years later, the sting still there. "We paid two years of punishment for something one of our former students did for two kids who couldn't play.

45

AN AMAZING TURNAROUND AT A&M

"The NCAA looked into a lot of players recruited in my class, and I can understand why. A&M was signing people from all over – out of Alabama, Colorado, Kentucky, Louisiana, New Mexico – and that kind of widespread recruiting was just unheard of at the time. But they never announced any infractions on anyone in my class."

Does that mean his class was all lily-white and pure? Probably not. But the under-the-table money was not having to be shipped into College Station from Fort Knox in armored trucks. Maybe a dollar here or there, but ...

"A lot of us never had much money," John David says, "so we were used to having to scrape by. If you were on an athletic scholarship, you couldn't hold a job during the school year.

"Well, I was married and had a baby, which means we had some pretty stiff doctor bills. I can tell you those bills got paid, but we weren't living it up. We didn't have a lot of cash lying around."

The Aggies figured somebody was picking on them, and they were probably right. There's no question Bryant's presence frightened other Southwest Conference coaches and supporters. George Sauer of Baylor and Jess Neely of Rice, in particular, had built perennial contenders under the current system of doing things.

Affable Abe Martin of TCU once joked that Bryant had forced other coaches to put away their golf clubs. In less than one year, Bear caused such a fuss that everyone else in the state began looking for ways to cut his legs out from under him – on the field or off.

Goehring says, "Most of the big-name national coaches seemed to like Coach Bryant and respect him, but most of the conference coaches hated him. He could be very arrogant and dominating."

Bryant spent more hours on the job than most of his peers, and in his spare time broke down game film. A few innovative coaches around the country were analyzing film; but, until Bryant came in from the outside, SWC coaches did not make a habit of it.

In effect, Bear forced the others to beware of his Aggies – and that really stuck in their craws. In the years

Mickey Herskowitz, interviewing John David (at left), would chronicle much of the Bryant era at Texas A&M.

leading up to Bear, A&M had increasingly become the butt of hundreds, thousands, of "Aggie jokes." Every day in every town in Texas, someone was telling the latest "how-many-Aggies-does-it-take-to-do-such-and-such" joke over a game of dominoes, a round of cocktails or a counter at a greasy-spoon restaurant. Outside of their own close-knit fraternity, the mere mention of "Aggies" prompted sneers and/or laughter around the state.

It seemed OK for the Aggies to be different, as long as they didn't make a lot of noise.

But when Bryant jarred all the experts by the depth and talent of his first recruiting class, he made their ears ring.

Long-distance operators around the state suddenly found themselves immersed, plugging in calls to the NCAA headquarters. They weren't using Ma Bell to swap Aggie jokes either.

NCAA investigators were dispatched into almost every hometown of every player in John David's freshman class. When they visited Springhill, Harry Crow threatened to feed one fellow a knuckle sandwich if he didn't watch out.

Goehring says, "We all knew players from other schools. Nothing went on at A&M that didn't go on anywhere else back then. Hell, we had proof; a number of our players were offered better deals elsewhere.

"But you have to remember what it was like, with the Aggies being the big joke around the state, then Coach Bryant arriving and all of a sudden stealing the whole spotlight. Other conference coaches were jealous, and Coach Bryant didn't care what they thought."

Bryant dryly observed that the penalty marked "the first time in NCAA history a school got put on probation after winning only one game (in 1954)."

But deep down, he felt the stab, and the hypocrisy made his skin crawl.

About all Bear could do was watch his team kick the others around on the field. And the Aggies did that, almost from the beginning of John David's three-year tenure as a starter.

In 1955, Bryant's "Team of Tomorrow" became known as "my bottle babies," and they would blend nicely with the Junction Boys.

CHAPTER FIVE

The Journey to Greatness at A&M Begins

John David Crow began rubbing shoulders with some of the legends of football long before he or any of the others – including Bear Bryant – would become on. Among those reporting with John David for fall workouts in 1955 were Bobby Joe Conrad, an acrobatic runner/receiver; Charlie Krueger, a tall, gangly tackle with great quickness; Jack Pardee, a fullback and inside linebacker who could drop a runner on a nickel and pick up an all-America award in change; and, Gene Stallings, a Junction Boy whose football credits would stretch very late into the 20th century, and perhaps beyond.

Dennis Goehring would be all-American in 1956, and Lloyd Hale an All-Conference center. Bryant dubbed Jim Stanley the meanest of his Aggies, and he said it fondly.

Bobby Drake Keith, Bobby Marks, Dee Powell, Don Watson, Roddy Osborne, Loyd Taylor, Jim Wright — the list of significant game contributors goes on.

In a quirk of scheduling, the Aggies' highly anticipated 1955 debut took place some 1,500 miles to the west, against UCLA, who happened to be the defending national champions.

Aggieland had been twirling its thumbs for 15 years in anticipation of a team with this much talent, and now most of the faithful would have to settle for newspaper accounts and radio news.

Early in the week leading up to the opener, a quiet, well-mannered newcomer to the varsity told a reporter, "We're ready to play."

Perhaps the writer detected the eagerness in John David's voice. Perhaps the writer anticipated hearing the eagerness and therefore did. Or, maybe it was just the best quote the scribe got all day.

Like most teammates, John David did not read the papers. Any papers. Players weren't afraid of what was being said, they just didn't find much interesting in all that gray print. Most players didn't even know where to buy a paper.

If you were going to fantasize about notoriety, you dreamed about the team being so good it would win a spot on a Movietone News newsreel at the picture show. Now that was news!

But Bear did read the papers and spotted Crow's comment. In practice that day, the big coach bellowed, "I can't read those damn press clippings anymore without seeing something in them I don't like!"

John David had no idea why Bryant was so mad but figured it had something to do with him. He asked A&M's sports information director, Jones Ramsey, if he could avoid as many interviews as possible.

"I just want to play football, that's all," John David pleaded. "I don't care about giving my opinion to anybody, especially if it's going to make Coach Bryant mad."

Bear's tongue, on the other hand, flapped free and easy, connected wirelessly to his brain. He almost al-ways said what he thought and usually it was as brutally direct and honest as a lead jab to the nose.

Other times, Bryant's grim, brusque replies carried softer messages that came through loud and clear.

The great Southern playwright of the time, Tennessee Williams, once wrote, "The violets in the mountains have broken the rocks." He could have been talking about Bear Bryant's voice.

In a press conference leading up to the 1955 opener, a Houston writer asked, "Coach, what's wrong with Crow's face?"

Bear explained the problem that occurred at delivery and the permanent paralysis, and the writer said it was a shame because John was a handsome young man otherwise.

Bryant replied almost poetically, "To me, he's handsome right now."

John David was not present to hear the exchange. But his early childhood nemesis, the one thing that made him fight people, had stopped being an issue long ago.

Here he was, sharing life with the sweetest gal he'd known. They were proud parents of a baby boy, who John David could make laugh. And he had hard-working teammates who loved the game the way he did, and who did not overly concern themselves with human frailties.

Goehring says, "It's kind of like the mole on your wife's cheek; once you've been around it awhile you stop paying it any attention."

A few years later, some Aggie alumni volunteered to help look into a plastic-surgery procedure that might relax the facial features. John David and Carolyn discussed the matter seriously.

For one thing, hot and humid football practices really messed with the eye that would not completely shut. Certain fields had a way of kicking up dust by the mops full. If the thing could be rectified, of course they wanted to look into it.

But when doctors in Houston ran a few nerve tests that failed to provide a solution, John David and Carolyn did not go home grief-stricken. Harry Crow had raised a proud, practical son – an admitted daddy's boy, through and through. John David did not care to fuss with the matter.

A&M's starters join Bryant and Lindsey Nelson (right) while listening to Red Grange prior to the 1955 Texas game.

When his teammates look back on John David's personality as a sophomore, the first thing many point out is his marriage. He practiced with them and ate meals on the training table with them; but, like the other handful of married players, he wasn't cutting up at night in the athletic dorms.

"Nobody was cutting up too much because Bryant wouldn't allow it," Krueger says. "If you ever partied a little, you damn sure better clean up in a hurry."

On occasion, John David did sneak off to the pool hall above the drugstore near campus. Through some of the wives, Carolyn heard that a few married players were hanging out when claiming to be studying at the library. She surprised John David there one afternoon, and he had a hard time hiding behind a pool stick when he knew he was supposed to have a book in his hand.

"It got real quiet when I walked in," Carolyn says. "A pool hall was no place for a woman back then."

All of 18 and quite petite, Carolyn froze her husband in front of everyone.

On their 43rd wedding anniversary, John David chuckled and said, "She came into that pool hall and told me to get my butt home to study. It wasn't so much the way she said as it was the look she gave me. And the fact she was even there.

"Carolyn forced me to study, sometimes by sitting down with me and making me do it. If anybody's name deserves to be on my diploma, it's hers."

But John David was not some rascal pup. He was confident, but not brash. He obviously didn't go to the pool hall to chase women. Or to drink (you had to drive across the Brazos River to reach the closest liquor stores; what establishments there were in College Station were dry). He could have fun, but he seldom lost focus.

Krueger says, "From the very beginning, he had a real presence that most people don't have. I mean, he was a real stud. You saw it when he walked in a room. He was just "growed up bigger' than most, if you know what I mean.

"One day this boy on the team from Southern Louisiana made some smart-ass comment to John, and all Crow said was, 'That's one. And you don't get a two.' That was it. The boy never bothered him again. The rest of us took notice real quick."

At A&M, John David never started a clique or joined one. His quiet, powerful leadership abilities would become even more noticeable later – once he was handed the ball on enough third and three's.

Jack Pardee, 1956 all-American fullback.

But like the other "bottle babies" in their sophomore year, John David was mostly just good and raw going into the opener against UCLA. Bryant wished to dispel any notions that his 1-9 Aggies of 1954 would be playing patsies to the national champs, who were returning three all-Americans.

Bear told reporters, "We're going out there in a big, four-motored plane. If we lose, we're coming back in a Greyhound bus."

John David and several other starters had never flown

across a pasture, let alone set sail for California in a prop-driven Delta bird that bucked every now and then while straining to reach the clouds. The bus from College Station to Houston and the Delta hitch-hike, cruising along at 250 mph, or thereabouts, consumed most of a day.

No geography course at any institution could have better taught those Aggies just how big their country is.

John David looked out the plane window and was awed by the tiny people down below, driving their tiny cars and trucks. But that wasn't as strange as looking around before kickoff at the 65,334 people gathered in one place, the Los Angeles Coliseum, making a noise unlike any John David and his teammates had heard.

In high school, you hear cheers – happy, peppy noises of glee. In college, you hear roars, waves of roars.

Long after retirement, most of the good ones can still hear the roars.

The eleventh of 12 children, Paul Bryant had grown up among more kin than neighbors, in a spot called Moro Bottoms, Arkansas. He wanted the trip to Los Angeles to be special for his small-town boys.

Each felt a foot taller even before boarding the bus to Houston. Bryant had seen to it that no matter how poor the player, he had a nice sports coat to wear. Some were introduced to a tailor for the first time.

The day following the flight, the Aggies toured Hollywood. Bryant introduced John David and the others to one of his former Alabama teammates, Johnny Mack Brown, a Western movie star of some renown.

Goehring says, "Most of us figured Coach Bryant could probably give old Johnny Mack acting lessons, but nobody said so out loud."

On the eve of the game, Bryant led those same unheralded rural boys into the Los Angeles Coliseum for a brief workout. Unlike John David, some had never played under lights, and Bryant had no idea how they might respond.

Pardee hailed from Christoval, a speck so lost among West Texas oilfields and tumbleweeds that his high school team played six-man football. Pardee ran well enough to score 57 touchdowns – his senior year alone – breaking whatever six-man records anyone bothered to keep.

Los Angeles and Christoval were roughly 50 years apart, and Jack Pardee was not the only one overwhelmed.

Years later, Pardee recalled walking into the Coliseum for that workout: "A lot of us tried to stay close to Coach Bryant for sheer comfort. We were scared witless, but we didn't dare let him see it, or know it. You don't ever, ever, let him know you're scared ... You can lose, but you can't be scared."

While running dummy plays during the light workout, Bear watched in horror as Pardee, his starting fullback, and Crow, his starting left halfback, smacked right into each other, without pads and helmets, head to head. Pardee claims to have been gazing around at the stadium and simply ran the wrong way.

For awhile, it appeared doubtful either back would play the next day. Bryant could not have been hotter had he swallowed a Roman candle.

But they did play, and Pardee admits he was more afraid of Bear Bryant than UCLA.

John David and five other sophomores started – six "bottle babies" and five Junction Boys – and the Aggies fought UCLA to a virtual stand-still in the trenches. But tailback Ronnie Knox came up with the game's three biggest plays, and the only touchdowns on three passes, for a 21-0 Bruins victory.

Afterward, sportswriter Melvin Durslag of The Los Angeles Examiner prodded Bryant, "You didn't really expect to beat them, did you?"

Bryant glared at Durslag indignantly and said, "You crazy fool. Why in hell do you think I came out here?"

Now the Aggies were 1-10 under Bear, and their loyal supporters were beginning to fidget again. Some were beginning to wonder aloud about this Paul Bryant fellow the days leading up to the one game John David

had circled on his schedule: A&M vs. LSU in Dallas' Cotton Bowl Stadium (occasionally, to attract bigger crowds, the Aggies played what would have been a home game in Dallas or Houston).

Other games in his career were bigger to John David from a team standpoint, but none would give him the personal satisfaction of that sophomore outing against his home state's darlings.

Yvonne, John David's little sister and Carolyn's good friend, was in her senior year at Springhill High, her third as a cheerleader. Along with seemingly everyone else in town, she listened to the A&M-LSU game on a car radio while cruising up and down Main at a snail's pace.

Springhill, La., rocked that night.

John David ripped off 130 yards on only 13 carries and scored two touchdowns in just his second game, leading the Aggies to a thorough 28-0 victory that equaled their win total the year before.

For only the second time in Bryant's 12 games as Aggie head coach, a player had rushed for more than 100 yards. In John David's three seasons, it would only happen twice more, once by him.

John David's most spectacular scamper resulted in his first collegiate touchdown – a 77-yarder, the longest run by an Aggie that season. He broke so many tackles it appeared LSU had too many men on the field.

As Bryant was still recalling 20 years later:

"We ran a trap play and both guards pulled and ran head-on into one another. Somehow Crow busted through the mess and ran (77) yards for a touchdown. He must have shook off 15 tackles, the greatest single run I ever saw.

"And when he came back to the bench, he patted everybody on the back: 'Great blocking, boys. Great blocking.' Ain't nobody blocked anybody, but he was giving them the credit. I knew then we were on our way."

Each time John David scored or did something special, all the car horns on Main in Springhill blared, carrying their celebration deeper into the tall, dark pines.

Yvonne says, "It was amazing. It seemed like everybody had their radios on that game, and everybody in town was honking horns."

John David lunges for extra yardage against UCLA, but it wasn't enough. A&M lost to the Bruins, 21-0.

Velma and Harry missed the town's big celebration because they were watching proudly, with Carolyn, from the Cotton Bowl stands. For the next month or so, they were quite the celebrities down at Tennyson's Drugs, where the soda fountain chatter on John David picked up considerably.

Famed Southwest Conference broadcaster Kern Tips, in that wonderful lilting manner of his, said John David had "announced his arrival on the Southwest Conference scene with the quiet modesty of an elephant stampede."

A mere two games into their sophomore seasons, the two most touted running backs of Bear's first crop already appeared headed in opposite directions: John Crow toward potential greatness, Ken Hall toward a disaster that Bryant later called the biggest

coaching mistake of his life.

But Bear liked the boys he had out there, and so did Aggies everywhere following a 21-3 romp over Houston and 27-0 whipping of Nebraska.

Opponents and members of the press were beginning to respect the Crow boy's knack of plowing over and through defenders. Fullbacks did that sort of thing, but not a halfback who could also scoot around end.

When John David did take a pitch and turn the corner, picking up steam on every stride, he did not feign or try to stutter past the defender coming up to close. He lowered a shoulder into the belly of a 160-pound defensive back and blew right over the guy – the runner punishing the tackler.

On defense, John David's presence was already beginning to loom like an eerie shadow over the other team's huddle. Opponents did not normally face a safety bigger than most college linemen.

You could run away from a lineman, but a safety was a different matter. This one could come up and flat out level a ball carrier, grinding the runner down like a cigarette butt, so that the next time the runner came through there he didn't seem to have that same gitty-up in his steps.

And as a lead blocker drawing a dead bead on a would-be tackler? Defenders were caught wide-eyed. His presence was frightening.

The Aggies were 3-1 going into their first serious showdown, a road game against Texas Christian, the conference favorites.

The Horned Frogs averaged 27.8 points a game in 1955, almost twice as many as anyone else in the conference, and they pummeled opponents by an 18.3 margin. They would go on to a 9-1 regular season and SWC title that gave them the Cotton Bowl bid. TCU finished No. 5 in the nation in The Associated Press poll, No. 6 in the UPI coach's poll.

But they did not beat the Aggies.

Recalling events that took place some 40 years into the past can be a bit iffy at times. John David credits Bryant for structuring his defense to slow Jim Swink. But Charlie Krueger insists the idea was Crow's, and that John David volunteered to stalk Swink.

Bear did practice John David all week as a rover whose primary responsibility was to shadow the left halfback on every down.

Then, at the very beginning of the game, John David was chopped down from behind and his knee stretched and twisted. A week's worth of planning was limping to the locker room.

Smokey Harper, the trainer, sent one of his assistants, Billy Pickard, to tape the knee up. But the room was locked, and Pickard led John David under the stands at Amon Carter Stadium, into a men's restroom, where he wrapped him tightly. As badly as John David yearned to play, he could not. And yet, if, as Krueger maintains, John David came up with the defense that stopped Jim Swink, he helped win a game without participating.

The Aggies' 19-16 victory was a real stunner, and no fluke. Nobody went into Fort Worth and knocked around an Abe Martin team like that, especially with one of your big hosses watching helplessly from the sidelines.

The victory sent a red-flare warning all over the Southwest Conference. These Aggies had arrived and looked like they were going to be in everybody's hair for a long time.

They hammered Baylor, 19-7, the next week and headed for The Hills of Arkansas a lofty 5-1 overall, 2-0 in the SWC. The Razorbacks were the defending conference champs. As it turns out, a victory would have given the Aggies the best record in conference play (despite a loss to Texas in the season finale).

Bryant kept his team in a hotel an hour away from Fayetteville. On the bus ride in, the players pointed out various signs on barn walls and cheerfully ribbed each other about their hometowns. A player in the rear said something funny and John David broke out laughing.

Bryant ordered the driver to pull the bus over.

"Since nobody's interested in playing today, why don't we all just go sit under a tree and have a picnic."

Nobody heard about or thought about a picnic the rest of the day.

Following a scoreless first half, Bryant was fussing around worse than Marilyn Monroe's hair stylist.

"We were in this very quiet room at halftime when all of a sudden the damn door almost blew off its latches," Krueger says. "Bryant stormed in, threw his hat down and hurled his coat across the room, and started grabbing guys and shaking them.

"He jerked up a lineman named Henry Clark by the shoulder pads. Henry must have weighed 235 pounds, and Bryant was shaking him like a rag doll and yelling, 'Henry, you ain't playin' worth a damn! You're gonna play better in the second half – right?'

"Henry kept going, 'Yes sir, yes sir.'

"Poor ol' Henry hadn't played a down."

The Aggies tied Arkansas, 7-7, that afternoon. Afterward, a reporter asked Bryant if playing the defending SWC champs dead-even on their home turf might qualify as a moral victory. At a time when hardly anyone had heard the expression, Bryant muttered, "A tie is like kissing your sister."

But this was still a young team spearheaded primarily by the "bottle babies." Evidence of their rawness came during their 13-2 victory over SMU in Game 8.

John David led the Aggies in kick-off returns that year with an 18.5 average, and he also handled punts. He pulled in a kick against SMU at his own 40 and tried to loop around end to avoid the oncoming wave of tacklers – only to be dropped 30 yards back, at the 10.

On the Aggies' next possession, Crow again gave ground trying to avoid the corner on an end sweep and lost five yards in the process. That's when he saw his sub, Bill Dendy, coming onto the field.

John David did not dare glance Bryant's way as he loped to the sidelines. His head down, he retreated to one end of the bench – as far from his coach as he could get.

He was nervous and knew what was coming, so he never looked up.

Then he noticed Bryant's shoes in front of him. Bear squatted and placed a hand on John David's knee, and said, "John, our goal is THATAWAY!"

Already that year, Bear had said, "John David gives so much of himself without regard for his physical well-being. He's got a chance to be the greatest player I've ever coached."

Praise like that only guaranteed that Bear would be driving him that much harder. In Game 9 at Rice, Bryant pulled John David in the fourth quarter, rendering one of his star players "dead" for the rest of the game. The Owls led, 12-0, with 3:40 remaining, and many of the 68,000 at Rice Stadium were heading for the exits.

But Loyd Taylor, Jim Wright, and Don Watson (Crow's sub) startled the Owls on a couple of big plays, and Gene Stallings plucked a vital on-side kick out of the air. The Aggies scored three touchdowns in a span of 2:18 and miraculously won, 20-12.

Afterward, Mickey Herskowitz found Bryant sitting on some steps near the locker room. Herskowitz had missed the entire comeback while stuck in a creeping press elevator taking a load of writers to the locker room at precisely the wrong time.

"What in the world happened out there, coach?" Herskowitz asked, bewildered.

"I don't know," Bear answered, shaking his head. "I was too busy praying."

The victories over SMU and Rice gave the Aggies a 7-1-1 record entering the season finale against arch-rival Texas. A&M had not lost since the opener to UCLA.

Now the probation was really stinging because Aggie faithful knew Bear's boys would have gotten a great bid, to either the Cotton Bowl by winning the conference or another bowl even if Texas beat them.

Bryant was so proud of his players, he promised them a trip to Honolulu to play the University of Hawaii – the Probation Bowl, he called it – if they beat the Longhorns. He was serious, too.

But the NCAA nixed the unscheduled trip, even before Texas took some of the glitter off the 1955 season with a 21-6 victory at Kyle Field.

When the game was still up for grabs, John David intercepted a pass and, two plays later, pulled in a 44-yard reception that Humble Oil radio broadcaster Tips Kern dubbed an "airmail special," setting up the lone score from a yard away.

Despite the sour finish, the Aggies were clearly back. All those bottle babies and Junction Boys would be together one more time in 1956. The anticipation was more than many could bear.

Even as a starter, John David carried the ball only 66 times as a sophomore, gaining 332 yards, averaging 5.0 a carry. He caught five passes for 101 yards and scored three touchdowns.

Perhaps more importantly, he had become a punishing defensive player. In the three years John David played at A&M, he says he cannot remember a time someone scored when he was the lone defender between the runner and the end zone. He grins and adds, "If it did ever happen, you're not going to hear me admit it."

From the day Carolyn pulled him out of the pool hall, his grades picked up. The young couple was adjusting to College Station, and to family life. The baby, little Johnny, was learning to walk and developing his own personality.

After that hectic, scary freshman year, maybe the Crows were going to be all right after all.

Crow reaches high to intercept a Longhorn pass intended for Ed Hawkins at the Aggie 20-yard line in 1955.

CHAPTER SIX

1956: A Season to Remember

John David might have looked dead to the student manager who first reached him. His big bones were sprawled out like an alley cat flattened by a school bus. This was the spring following John David's excellent sophomore season, and Bear Bryant was pushing his boys toward new limits.

Jupiter, if possible.

He had also devised a way to avoid potential headaches with the Aggie alumni.

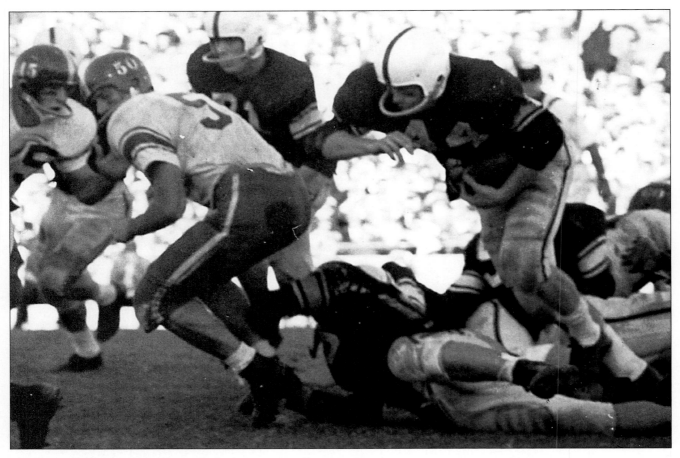

John David (44) rips off tackle against Rice at Kyle Field in 1956. The Aggies would eventually win, 21-7.

About an hour before John David passed out, Bear's whistle blew a halt to a particularly rigorous practice. Bryant smiled at the alumni sprinkled in the bleachers and gently wished them good riddance – to Mars, if possible – as his exhausted football squad clomped into the locker room.

John David peeled off his soggy uniform and found a metal folding chair to take with him to the showers. He placed the chair directly under a shower head and flopped down, prepared to let the water splatter his aching muscles the remainder of the Eisenhower presidency.

Suddenly, when a manager stuck his head around the corner and yelled, "Put 'em back on!"

The manager could have announced an outbreak of smallpox and not caused more coughing and fumbling around. Only three months earlier, for chrissakes, these

guys had looked stronger than the Budweiser Clydesdales – and perhaps just as effective when it came to lifting the spirits of Aggies everywhere.

"You're crazy!" John David snapped at the student manager, chastising the messenger because Western Union was a little too big.

The manager looked at John David as if to say, "Um, excuse me, but you're the football player and I'm not," but instead intoned, "The man said to put 'em back on."

When the 1956 Aggies-to-be returned listlessly to the field, Bear Bryant told them to kneel around him.

"I couldn't do it," John David says, "I knew if I dropped down, I'd never get up."

For two football seasons, he had watched so many others pack their modest suitcases and tearfully depart. At 17 and 18, many had been Friday night heroes, not only of their towns but of their districts and states. At 19 and 20, they were kissing off their scholarships and walking away from a game many of them really did love because Bear Bryant drove his teams that far.

Enough of them disappeared that they could have filled the starting lineups of every squad in the Southwest Conference, with key backups to spare.

Now, with the alumni sauntering home from the stands and his drained players before him, Bryant explained how great they could be in the fall – but only if they worked hard enough.

And speaking of work, how's about a little scrimmage?

"I just looked at him, framed by the tunnel in the north end of the stadium," John David says. "And I told myself, 'By God, you might kill me, but you are not going to run me off!'

"I woke up three hours later in the infirmary. I'd had a heat stroke."

When John David opened his eyes, he had an orange drink in one hand and Carolyn's fingers in the other. Bear Bryant stood at the foot of the bed and, after the three of them nodded at each other and silently thanked their lucky stars, Bryant drawled, "Hell, John David, if you were tired, why didn't you just tell me?"

From his home near San Francisco, Charlie Krueger brought up that moment more than 40 years old. He and some of the other players had showered and rushed to the infirmary to check on John David. They had watched Bear Bryant pace around the waiting room, trying to keep distress off his face, smoking as if the entire state of Texas might be running out of Chesterfield's at any moment.

"I think it scared the hell out of him that he'd almost killed John David," Krueger says. "He was watching one of his favorite players take saline and glucose injections into his veins. Coach Bryant didn't show any emotions, but I think we all knew it was a very serious moment for him."

Maybe the scare gave Bear an excuse to relax some and actually embrace one of his players – verbally, anyway, and only on occasion. For whatever the reasons, a mutual admiration was struck up between the two that surely is among the more heartfelt player/coach relationships in the history of college football.

Bryant damn near adopted John David simply by calling him John David.

Krueger says, "The old man did like John. You could see it. But none of the rest of us resented it. It's kind of like we all figured, 'Damn, if he's gonna pick a favorite, he picked a good one.' "

They certainly had their similarities. John David may have been a good 20 years younger, which means he'd yet to weather a Depression or fight a war, but their rural backgrounds and physical stature, their fierce pride and astonishing fear of failure, their willingness to dig however deep down it took – why, they were twins.

In life, Bryant never understood the back-of-the-bus passengers; he preferred someone willing to take the wheel every now and then. If he could have chosen a group to drive him around the world, it probably would have been the Junction Boys. Maybe one of his national championship teams later at Alabama, but probably the Junction Boys.

But if he needed just one driver? Even his Alabama all-Americans – Joe Namath and Johnny Musso and Kenny Stabler and roughly five dozen others – probably know the answer.

The wives, Mary Harmon and Carolyn, also played magical roles in it all. They, too, were 20 years apart, yet very much in tune.

Of course, the surroundings had something to do with it. Mary Harmon and Carolyn had arrived in College Station at roughly the same time. They didn't know any more about Texas than they did about Disneyland – which had just opened in California.

Imagine two women, both pretty in pink, getting off a stagecoach in Frontierland when they were anticipating red-carpet treatment at the Enchanted Castle.

"We had a great friendship," Carolyn says. "And Mrs. Bryant really fell in love with our son, Johnny. She'd call us on the phone out of the blue and ask if we'd like to bring Johnny over so she could play with him. Or she'd come by and get him, and she'd keep him until Coach Bryant came home."

Little Johnny Crow would spot Mary Harmon and break into a smile bigger than a football, and his little hands would reach for her the way they did for his parents.

Twenty years later, he'd be playing at Alabama for Bryant.

Before the start of the fall semester in '56, an Aggie built three four-plex apartment houses near campus. He asked Bryant if he would like a piece of the action, and Mary Harmon campaigned for Carolyn as the on-premise manager.

"That way," Mary Harmon explained, "she can hold a job and still be around Johnny."

The Crow family traded in their barracks at the College View Apartments and moved to the newer digs for their final two years at A&M.

"Our rent was something like $33 a month at College View," John David says. "That included utilities, and it was furnished. We paid $25 a month at the new place, even though Carolyn ran it, but we also paid utilities plus had to put half the money down on some used furniture."

About the time the Crows settled in to their new digs, another season was on them.

In May of 1956 at a meeting in Fayetteville, the Southwest Conference lifted its probation off Texas A&M, making the Aggies eligible for the league championship.

Now, if the NCAA would follow suit, the Aggies had a chance of being bowl-bound.

In the meantime, there were these tackling dummies waiting in the heat and humidity. Bryant's heart may have softened on John David, but he wasn't about to change his methods for anybody – including John David.

Bryant would actually assume the three-point stance and go head-to-head with his players.

"He was big, and he would get down there and just knock your chops off," Krueger says. "One time, this big ol' boy got the better of him, and the kid left him on the ground and started walking away, figuring he was bound to be kicked off the team for whipping the coach. Bryant yelled at him to come on back. That's what he had been looking for."

Others, Bryant let walk. They were sneaking out of College Station the way those before them had left Junction. Enough so, that it genuinely surprised Bryant when a player appeared at his office instead of lurking off.

"When we were freshmen, Jim Stanley and I bet each other a fifth of whiskey who would last longer," Krueger says. "We weren't joking. But we knew if we ever made

the break, he would never have us back. He told us that many times."

Krueger did get his fill of Bryant following his freshman year. He had selected A&M because the college was only a half-hour's drive from his hometown, Caldwell. After Bryant showed him the way to hell and back a few times, Krueger decided to transfer to Texas A&I, also nearby in Kingsville.

"All my childhood, I heard sermons on the importance of being God-fearing," Krueger says. "But I never actually saw God in Caldwell. Bryant was right there in front of me, and he was real. I wasn't sure God would actually kill me, but I knew Bryant damn sure could.

"I feared him a whole lot more than I feared God."

Krueger was working a summer job at the Houston ship channel with Dennis Goehring, Dee Powell, Jim Stanley, and a few others, when he stuffed his clothes and extras into a pasteboard box and headed for Kingsville.

Goehring and two assistant coaches, Jim Owens and Willie Zapalac, volunteered to bring him back. Eventually, the coaches gave up, but Goehring remained and four days later convinced Krueger to return.

"Bryant sent an airplane to pick us up, and we were taken directly to his house," Goehring recalls. "He was very fatherly, and he told Charlie, 'You're going to be an all-American, I guarantee you, because we're going to be a winning football team and you're going to be a big part of it.' "

Krueger was skeptical, whether he showed it or not.

"Even then," Krueger says, "I figured he was just setting me up so that he could humiliate me in front of everybody in practice. But before we left his house, he said, 'I don't want to ever discuss this again.' And he never brought it up or used it against me."

Kenneth Hall was not as fortunate. His pleasant demeanor clashed with the coach's yearning for hell-bent enthusiasm. Where Bear Bryant's fear tactics and constant prodding instilled a positive burning in the guts of players like John Crow and the Junction Boys, those same methods bewildered Hall.

Hall had decided to attend Texas A&M long before Bryant was hired. He went from singing in his church choir one month to feeling the blues under Bryant the next.

Goehring says, "Kenneth Hall was the guy everybody

John David (44) romps through the LSU secondary in A&M's 9-6 win against the Tigers in Baton Rouge in 1956.

thought would win the Heisman. He was our superstar, even bigger and stronger than Crow.

"But Coach Bryant did not dote over anybody. Everyone knew Crow and Krueger were among his chosen few, but he didn't cut them any slack. He tended to respect guys who stood up to him every now and then. He wanted to see you get mad when he pushed you. That wasn't Ken's makeup. He just never openly showed the hunger Coach Bryant demanded on defense. If Ken had fired back at him just once ...

"I used to pick fights in practices just to get the attention of the coaches," Goehring explained. "Seriously, anytime Coach Bryant walked past a field I was practicing on, I'd whack the guy across me upside the head. I think

it helped me move up from the seventh team to the first."

Bryant must have figured if he couldn't force Hall to get mad, he'd use him as an example to everyone else.

For all of spring training and in the fall until the first game in 1956, Bryant's Aggies christened each practice with the "Challenge Drills." A player would notify the coaches earlier in the day that he wanted to challenge the guy ahead of him on the roster. (If, for example, a fourth-string tackle wanted to move up to the third team, all he had to do was beat No. 3 in the challenge drill).

"Once the season started," Pardee says, "we were graded by film. But at other times, anybody could challenge anybody ahead of him."

First one player would run the ball or block the other, depending on the position in limbo, and then they'd reverse sides and do it again, over and over, until one clearly prevailed.

Another aspect of the challenge was known as "The Gauntlet." Bryant would line four defenders between two dummies and order the ball carrier to run through them. The drill didn't end until the runner succeeded.

Ken Hall is not likely to ever forget the drill.

Hall says, "Sometimes he'd walk through the locker room and announce to everybody, 'OK, so-and-so on the fifth team has challenged Hall. Let's go!'

"And we'd go out there and, with everybody standing around watching, he'd line up four guys, and they'd beat my brains out. And that was before practice."

Hall never started a game at Texas A&M. He never even lettered.

He quit the first time halfway through the sophomore season of the "bottle babies." John David volunteered to retrieve him and succeeded in bringing him back.

Six games into 1956, Ken Hall left again. And again, John David asked if he could go find him. This time Bryant said no.

In his autobiography, *Bear*, he admits, "It's easy to say (Hall) did this or that, but what about me? My job was to get him to play and I didn't. So there's no doubt in my mind that I failed... Ken Hall was a fine young man, and he was worth saving."

In 1957, Edmonton of the Canadian Football League gave Hall a $7,000 contract and $700 to cover moving expenses.

John David Crow and Kenneth Hall had been the Golden Boys on the Team of Tomorrow. Now, during what should have been their golden years, one was gone.

"I tried to keep up with them while I was in Canada but it was tough to do," Hall says. "I mean, A&M was my school, and I really cared a lot about John Crow and Bobby Joe Conrad and Ed Dudley and a lot of others.

"I still don't understand why it all happened. There were days when the assistant coaches guaranteed I'd be starting that Saturday, and I wouldn't play a down. I knew where the goal line was and how to get there, but I never got the ball."

Some dozen years later, his playing days long over, Kenneth Hall drove alone one night from Sugar Land to College Station to attend an A&M alumni banquet. He didn't see anyone there he recognized, except for the guest speaker, Alabama coach Paul Bryant.

"He looked tired, and much, much older," Hall says. "After he spoke, I found him at a table signing a few autographs. I walked up to him and stuck out my hand, and he looked up – I mean, he looked me right in the eyes – but he didn't put the pen down. He just said, 'I know you.' That was it.

"He never shook my hand, and neither one of us said another thing. I got in my car and drove off. It was like closing the book. I guess it was just one more incident that showed me maybe I'd been right to leave."

In August 1997, the first annual Ken Hall Celebrity Golf Classic was staged in Fredericksburg, a small town west of Austin in the Texas Hill Country.

Some 26 former pro players showed up, including John David. Proceeds from the event would help set up a college scholarship each year "for a middle of the road kid with a lot of get up and go," Hall explains.

Though he was talking of selling the place, Hall has owned and operated a barbecue restaurant in Fredericksburg for the last decade. He watches the local high school team on Friday nights, and some of the players drop by for ribs and hot links during the week.

On one of the shelves overlooking his customers is a bottle of Hall's Barbecue Sauce. Right next to it is a Bear Bryant Coca-Cola bottle.

"It's my way of saying it's OK," Hall says. "We were both young, and we both made mistakes. I don't understand some of it, but the only logical explanation I have is that the chemistry between us was wrong. There's no other answer."

John David shakes his head and says, "Ken Hall was the best football player on this campus, bar none. If we had both gone to Oklahoma, where Bud Wilkinson's coaching style would have better suited Ken's personality, I imagine he would have been a great player and I would have been second fiddle to him."

But this wasn't Bud. This was Bear.

"Some things sound cruel and barbaric today, but I didn't find them all that brutal at the time because things were a lot different," John David says.

THE TEXAS A&M AGGIES 1956

LLOYD HALE — ALL-CONFERENCE

'56 SOUTHWEST CONFERENCE CHAMPIONS

JOHN CROW — ALL-CONFERENCE

JOHN TRACEY — ALL-CONFERENCE

DENNIS GOEHRING — ALL-CONFERENCE

Coached by PAUL (BEAR) BRYANT and his fine staff!

· SCORES ·

AGGIES	OPPONENTS	
19	VILLANOVA	0
9	L.S.U	6
40	TEXAS TECH.	7
14	HOUSTON	14
7	T.C.U	6
19	BAYLOR	13
27	ARKANSAS	0
33	S.M.U.	7
21	RICE	7
34	TEXAS	21

REMEMBER JUNCTION! THESE GUYS WEAR THE HEART OF THIS GREAT AGGIE TEAM: LOCKETT, KEITH, STALLINGS, GOEHRING, PARDEE, WATSON, POWELL AND HALE.

CHARLES KRUEGER — ALL-CONFERENCE, ALL-AMERICA · INS·

RODDY OSBORNE — ALL-CONFERENCE

JACK PARDEE — ALL-CONFERENCE, ALL-AMERICA LOOK MAGAZINE.

"I feared losing more than I enjoyed winning. So did other guys. Losing humiliated me; people treated you differently. Coach Bryant's methods – the reasons he did push us to the edge – are what made us ultimately win. Some people didn't want any part of it, and it was their right to leave; but those of us who stayed grew to really appreciate Coach Bryant."

His was the hard-fought, clinched-jaw mentality brought back from overseas in World War II. Toughness permeated every walk of life, and dominated football fields.

"Coach Bryant used to say when you cross that line, you went to work and played football the way the game was meant to be played," John David says. "And once you crossed back over the line, you were to conduct yourself as a gentleman.

"He was tough and mean on the football field, but as a man he had a very tender heart. In a lot of ways, he was a big pushover. He'd cry openly. He said there was no shame in showing your feelings."

Later at Alabama, Paul Bryant came to realize that not everyone who left him was a quitter. Some simply found a different approach more appealing.

But those who did stay and endure at Texas A&M soon discovered what all the fuss was about.

It was about winning. Or not losing.

CHAPTER SEVEN

Glory Returns to Aggieland

That spring of 1956, as doctors at the A&M infirmary pumped fluids into John David's weary veins, baseball training camps were in full swing all over Florida.

The New York Yankees were again stocked with talent, including a right-hander acquired a year earlier in an 18-player swap. The right-hander had already led the American League in two categories: losses (thanks to a 3-21 record with Baltimore in '54) and cocktail consumption. He drank enough liquor that spring to carry on a high romance with Fort Lauderdale's 4 a.m. barroom closing time.

Gene Stallings, an All-SWC end in 1956, from Paris, Tex.

One early morning, the pitcher smacked his car into a telephone pole. Casey Stengel, his skipper, shrugged to reporters and allowed, "He musta been out mailing a letter."

Only two weeks before Texas A&M met TCU in an October showdown of Homeric scope, Stengel took a chance with his World Series starting rotation and asked his mailman to deliver a championship. In reply, Don Larson hurled the one and only perfect game in World Series history.

To many Americans, the day was memorable for two reasons. The perfect game, obviously. And the fact each game of that World Series was broadcast live on television.

Many great moments of the era were not captured live on camera. Bobby Morrow became America's Olympic darling that summer, thanks mostly to newspaper and radio accounts, game films, and hearsay.

In pro football headlines: Bobby Layne, a Texan who could out-throw and out-drink Don Larson, led pro football in points scored while quarterbacking and kicking for the Detroit Lions. Also in 1956, the NFL installed a new rule, making it illegal to grab any player's face mask – other than the ball carrier's.

The one game ultimately recognized for popularizing pro football on television, the Baltimore Colts' double-overtime playoff victory over the New York Giants, was still two years away.

And this just in from other sports: Floyd Patterson, a year younger than John Crow, whips Archie Moore for the heavyweight title of the world; and, the Philadelphia Warriors have beaten the Ft. Wayne Pistons for the NBA title!

This wasn't ESPN's SportsCenter. This was, "Extra, extra, read all about it!" This was Kern Tips on the radio and your own imagination filling in the blanks.

Wilt Chamberlain, a 7-foot sophomore in 1956 at the University of Kansas, would not stun pro basketball by scoring 100 points in one night for another five-and-a-half years; and, there weren't any live television cameras in Hershey, Pa., that night either.

For Bear Bryant, what could have been more perfect? Everyone else in the country could only hear about how good his Aggies had become. News by word-of-mouth

can be the eeriest of all. And if the NCAA did not lift what Bear deep-down felt to be an unjust probation, nobody would be seeing them in a bowl game either.

How good were the 1956 Aggies?

So good that five of the eleven starters played at least 10 years of professional football: Bobby Joe Conrad, Charlie Krueger, Jack Pardee, John Tracey, and John Crow.

So good that, at a time when the Southwest Conference talent pool ran as deep as any in the nation, only four players from anywhere else made the league's various first-team All-SWC squads with any regularity.

Seven Aggies joined them: Crow, Pardee and quarterback Roddy Osborne in the backfield; Lloyd Hale at center; Goehring at guard; Krueger at tackle; and, Tracey at end.

"We could stomp with the best of them," Krueger says. "We punished teams with our defense, and then we turned around and punished their defenses with our offense."

That's not to imply Bear Bryant's third group of Aggies glided through 10 tangos without so much as dirtying their nails. Most games were low-scoring brawls settled in the fourth quarter, often late – the way Bryant liked it.

The overriding emphasis on his game plan remained fairly simplistic, but not all that easy to carry out: Beat 'em while they're up, until they'd rather stay down.

Only once did an opponent score first in the second half. Bryant liked that, too.

He probably could not have enjoyed Texas A&M's first Southwest Conference championship since 1941 any other way.

Bud Wilkinson's Oklahoma Sooners won the national championship that year. Tommy McDonald, the little halfback whose skittish, water-bug spurts had cooled John David on the idea of going there, was the star attraction on an 11-0 squad.

The Aggies finished fifth nationally in both polls. But most sane coaches and players in the country, given their druthers, would have probably taken their chances against Oklahoma.

Tennessee (10-0) and Miami (8-0-1) were the only

In 1956, A&M won the Southwest Conference title with a record of 9 wins and one tie, but were unable to play in the Cotton Bowl on New Year's Day because of NCAA sanctions.

other NCAA teams to go undefeated in 1956; but, after the bowls, only Oklahoma and Texas A&M remained that way.

Halfway through the season, sportswriters began worming through the crowds at Kyle Field, quizzing old-timers about who was better, Jarrin' John Kimbrough from the last great era or Jarrin' John Crow from this one.

A Houston Post survey found 10 of the most knowledgeable rail birds equally divided on the subject. Of course, John David still had the remainder of 1956 and all of '57 to go.

By then, everybody knew Crow was the sledgehammer on the team you'd least likely want to be introduced to at such times as coin flips, and thereafter.

The lone blemish on the '56 record was a 14-14 tie to Houston in Game 4, and the Aggies probably would have won it, too, if Bear had elected to kick a field goal – from the one-yard line – on the game's final play.

"I don't remember anyone on the team questioning that decision at the time," John David says. "Mainly because we didn't question him about anything."

Perhaps to Bryant, a field goal simply wasn't the manly way to settle a day filled with more brutal collisions than a Crazy 8 demolition derby. It's the symphony lover who's thrilled by the crashing of cymbals; Bear's ears ached for some of that human thunder.

Bobby Drake Keith, one of his Junction Boys starting at end, had his jaw broken that day. On the tamer side were an assortment of bloody lips and bruised knuckles.

Houston's Cougars, who would go on to win the Missouri Valley Conference, led 14-7 and were sitting pretty when a splendid punt died on the A&M five-yard line. The Aggies, not prone to pass, were staring at four minutes of clock and 95 yards of real estate.

They covered 94 and had a play to go.

"It would have been a cinch field goal for Loyd Taylor," Bryant later recounted, shouldering the blame.

Legally anyway, coaches couldn't call plays. But they did determine whether to kick or go for it on fourth down, indicating their preference by whether they threw the kicking tee onto the field or not (Sometimes Bear, and surely others, would place a strip of tape on the bottom of the tee if he wanted the kick faked).

Just before that last play, Bryant did send in Don Watson with the tee, to give to Taylor for the winning attempt. But then Bryant changed his mind and called Watson back to the sidelines.

Field goals were not the automatic chip shots they are today, but still ...

You had to figure Bear was more interested in the manly approach. It simply wasn't in his makeup to go to war for 59 minutes and then allow the outcome to be determined by the accuracy of a wobbly kick.

"I figured with Pardee and Crow, we ought to be able to get a yard," Bear said.

They would have needed the ball.

Pardee did not lose yardage on one carry – not only that season but in his entire career at A&M. The Houston Post named him Most Valuable Player in the Southwest Conference that year. Crow was already the team's short-yardage answer to Mighty Mouse.

Instead, Roddy Osborne, gritty beyond his abilities, kept the ball and tried to skirt end. A block was missed, and another sister was kissed. Other than wives and weekend dates, the tie left the only hickey on the Aggies all year.

They dropped from an early No. 9 ranking in the country to No. 14.

But the Aggies didn't have any time to sulk. Next up was TCU, still showcasing the magic of Jim Swink, second in the Heisman voting the year before to Ohio State's Howard (Hopalong) Cassady.

The Frogs hungered to amend their only loss of the year before. They were ranked No. 4 nationally after smothering Kansas, Arkansas and Alabama by a combined 96-12 score. Even though the game would be played at sold-out (42,000) Kyle Field in College Station, the Frogs were 14-point favorites.

College football experts figured if someone managed to upset Oklahoma that year, the A&M-TCU game could very well be for the national championship.

The contradictions in the makeup of the two teams were dramatic: Bear Bryant's Patton-like approach vs. Abe Martin's gentler, philosophical lean; John David Crow's bullish romps vs. Jim Swink's Houdini acts; one of college football's premier defenses vs. one of the great offensive units.

A contingent that included Carolyn and her parents, as well as Velma and Harry Crow, walked into the stadium that day dressed to the hilt – the women in their prettiest hats and bonnets, the men as distinguished as the President's cabinet.

The Presidential race between Gen. Dwight Eisenhower and Adlai Stevenson was also headed to the wire. Just that morning, Eisenhower accused his Democratic opponent of "speaking incredible folly" when Stevenson called the military draft a waste of manpower and money.

The Cadets were ready for a rumpus.

During warm-ups, the Aggies' famous mascot dog, Reveille, bit the leg of TCU assistant coach Walter Roach. Every man, woman, and animal was pumped.

"We went out to warm up and it was hot and muggy," John David says. "Then we went into our meeting room and Coach Bryant started telling us how absolutely nothing should distract us – not even if a blizzard or hurricane came through.

"I was sitting there sweating and wondering, 'What in the world is he talking about?'"

Just before kick-off, a few clouds floated along the blue skies over Kyle Field and the lightest of sprinkles fell.

"I thought, 'Thank God! What a relief!'" Krueger says. "Nobody wanted to play in that heat and humidity."

Chuck Curtis, TCU's talented quarterback, completed his first six passes and Swink appeared too nimble.

Then, early in the second quarter during a 73-yard TCU drive, the skies grew darker than a high school library and the rains came.

And came and came and came.

It was the kind of rain you might find in a Western movie with Walter Brennan or Gabby Hayes navigating the chuck wagon through a cattle stampede.

The game, of course, went on ...

Wind gusts were clocked at 90 to 120 miles an hour, howling like so many sailors on leave, horizontal sheets of rain potent enough to capsize 24 boats in Galveston Bay 150 miles to the southeast. Flagpoles bent to near 90-degree angles, and the light stands shook like a troupe of bad belly dancers. The Cadets stood firmly in the stands.

After being rain-soaked, John David put on jersey No. 84 at halftime. He would score the Aggies' only TD in a 7-6 win.

And the game went on ...

"Ponchos throughout the stands were flapping around and blowing everywhere," Carolyn says. "But it never entered our minds to leave that game."

And on ...

The cleanup crew counted 5,000 ladies' hats beneath the stands. Word reached the press box that 10 private planes at Easterwood Airport had been blown over, and almost 100 had been damaged. Writers could not see the action from the press box. Officials had to hold the ball in place between snaps, and for awhile small chunks of hail splattered helmets, making signals virtually impossible to hear.

Jim Swink once recalled, "The wind was blowing so hard you could barely breathe. You had to turn your head sideways. It was almost impossible to hear. Visibility was zero."

Because his eye could not completely close, the conditions bordered on unbearable for John David.

"It (the eye) always seemed to collect trash on a normal day," he says. "But this was not what you'd call a normal day."

Krueger, 6-5 and 215 lbs., says, "I actually had to lean my body into the wind to reach the huddle. It was wild, and most starters on both teams played about 56 of the 60 minutes."

TCU's long march continued through the storm, so thoroughly rocking the Aggies back on their heels that the Frogs set up first-and-goal at the A&M 2.

Swink scored, but an off-sides penalty rubbed it out and set up an eventual fourth-and-goal from the two.

Ken Wineburg, the conference's leading rusher to date, fumbled a yard shy of the goal as the Aggies, hurricane winds in their faces, were hauling him down.

But Roddy Osborne coughed up the ball at the A&M eight, and TCU came knocking again on third and goal from the three. The skies were completely blackened as Pardee and Crow keyed on Swink and guessed right, dropping Swink right at the line. The closest official did not raise his arms, and instead placed the ball an inch short.

Again the ball was handed to Swink, and again Pardee stuffed him short. TCU thought Swink had scored both times. Abe Martin was so mad he left his angry Frogs on the sidelines and ran onto the field. Swink leaped up and down, screaming into the wind.

As Associated Press scribe Will Grimsley put it, "Abe Martin rushed in from the sidelines to throw his voice into the dissent. It mattered not."

Three times the Aggies had mounted goal-line stands. Three times, the Frogs could have kicked, but the storm made a field goal a high risk. The half ended scoreless.

Just to get into a dry uniform, John David switched jersey numbers at halftime, from his standard 44 to William Appelt's No. 84.

In the second half, the storm weakened. Twice the Frogs drew close enough to attempt field goals from 16 and 23 yards, both going awry. But later in the third quarter, TCU recovered an Osborne fumble only 29 yards shy of the goal.

GLORY RETURNS TO AGGIELAND

From the 13, Swink hit Jim Shofner with a sure touchdown pass, but Shofner could not hang on to the slick ball. On fourth down from the 11, Curtis surprised the Aggies, faking to Swink and drilling a pass to O'Day Williams, who plucked the ball out of the air with one hand and fell into the end zone.

Although the extra point was missed, TCU finally led, 6-0, and seemed to have gotten over the psychological barrier of not being able to dent the Aggie goal line.

Back came TCU in the fourth period. Curtis whipped a sure touchdown to Shofner in the end zone, but 150-pound Don Watson, the Aggies' do-everything handyman, jumped higher, perhaps, than he ever had, and came up with the interception for a touchback that kept the Aggies within six.

Watson's heroics pumped up the Aggies. They had 80 yards to go, and most of the fourth quarter to pull off an upset that would impact the national rankings – if they could ever get untracked. The sun even came out.

Bryant had installed an option play that week that he learned from OU's Wilkinson – a quick flip, run or pass play with the halfback having the option. But the conditions had prevented him from using it until late.

Now, he called for it.

First, John David turned the corner and ran 21 yards to the Aggie 41. Two plays later, Crow faked a dive into the line and Osborne gave it to Watson, who followed a Ken Beck block 37 yards to the TCU 20.

Crow banged inside for three and darted outside for another 13, then at top speed crashed through the Frogs for a first down at the four. But TCU stiffened, forcing a third and goal at the eight. Because of the conditions and Bear's disdain for gimmicks, the Aggies had not passed all day.

Nor did Osborne pass this time. He pitched to Watson, who, hemmed in the backfield, fired a touchdown pass to John David wide open in the end zone.

The sun now shining brightly, Loyd Taylor booted the extra point, and the Aggies were up, 7-6, with nine minutes left.

That's the way the Hurricane Game ended. One pass. One touchdown. One major upset.

Wineburg managed just 13 yards on eight carries.

Swink a more respectable 82 but on 24 carries, a 3.4 average. John David led the Aggies with 70 yards on nine carries. Osborne kept 17 times for another 54.

Goehring was voted the outstanding lineman of the game. Pardee, playing despite a badly injured shoulder, made 13 tackles.

The writers asked Bryant, "Did it go according to plan?"

"No," Bear replied, "it went according to prayer."

He paused and said, "There's never been a team with more guts." Then he excused himself, explaining, "I need to get out of these wet clothes. I don't want to die if I can help it, although this would be a good time."

Bear walked across campus on his way home with his 10-year-old son, Paul Jr., at his side. He said he just wanted to let it all soak in again.

The Frogs did not enjoy the prick of defeat. The Fort Worth Star-Telegram ran several articles proclaiming that TCU "movies" showed Swink scoring at least on third down, and perhaps fourth, too.

John David grins these many years later and says, "I was right down there in it, and I'll go to my grave telling people he didn't score. That's what they called."

Incredibly, the next week the Aggies played Baylor in what both Bear and John David called the bloodiest, meanest, roughest game either witnessed – ever.

Jack Pardee did not start because of a separated shoulder. But he eventually entered the game anyway because it hurt less to play than to watch from the sidelines.

"At one point," Crow says, "there was a big fracas near their bench, and I got kicked hard in the helmet. In all my games in high school and college, and later in the pros, I can think of only one time when I knew someone was intentionally trying to hurt me. That was when one of the Washington Redskins tried to hit me with his fist.

"The pros were bigger and more skilled, but nobody played both ways there. That Baylor game was the toughest. Second-toughest was the high school game against Byrd my senior year, when we came back to tie."

John David threw a touchdown pass to Tracey, the sophomore end. And Osborne hit Watson for another TD. But the score was knotted at 13 on fourth down from six yards out when John David bellowed in the huddle, "Give me the cock-eyed ball, and I'll put it in there."

They did and he did, busting free, and the Aggies won, 19-13.

Bobby Joe Conrad, maybe the most gifted all-around athlete on the team, says, "When we needed the toughest yards, especially the real important third and two's and third and three's, John David would get it. Because when the game came down to it, he would put his shoulder down and drive and get the yards."

From there, it was clear sailing to the finale against Texas. The Aggies ripped Arkansas, 27-0; SMU, 33-7; and, Rice, 21-7, making them 8-0-1.

Aggies all over the state were thumping their chests, and Corps members had a little extra pep in their step when they performed their traditional march in the downtown Dallas parade before the SMU game.

They marched in perfect cadence, saluted at precisely the right times, and then chanted, firmly and proudly:

Jack and Jill went up the hill,
She won't do it but her sister will;
Where's she from?
SMU!

On Nov. 13, 1956, between the victories over SMU and Rice, the NCAA met and considered lifting the probation. Other SWC members came to the Aggies' defense. Abe Martin at TCU, whose Frogs most benefited from the NCAA's refusal, said, "The ruling stymies one of the top bowl teams in the country."

Because of the NCAA's decision, TCU represented the SWC in the Cotton Bowl, squeaking past Jimmy Brown and Syracuse, 28-27; and, Baylor edged Tennessee in the Sugar Bowl, 13-7. For their "bowl game" the Aggies would have to settle for a victory over the Texas Longhorns on Thanksgiving Day.

But the Aggies had never beaten Texas in Austin. Not once, in the 50-plus year history of the most bitter rivalry in the Southwest Conference.

Every year, everybody within hearing distance of the Humble network could eat their turkey and rub their bellies and listen to Kern Tips describe the tantalizing ac-

tion – on the radio, where the mind still had an imagination.

The Thanksgiving of '56, those hated tea-sippers were the one obstacle between the Aggies and an undefeated season.

However, doctors worried that John David may have broken his foot during the Rice game. It looked like a clown's balloon as he hobbled to practice all week. There was great concern among students in conversations at the Memorial Student Center.

What if he couldn't play?

When a reporter asked John David if X-rays had been taken, Crow answered, "There's no use in it; I'm going to play anyway." He couldn't stand the thought that a doctor might put the foot in a cast.

As always, the Cadets draped bed sheets and huge, self-made signs out their dormitory windows – some with slogans encouraging the Aggies to kick the Bevo out of Texas, some wishing players like Crow and Pardee good health, and some just too damn raunchy to mention.

That week's bonfire glowed like an arsonists' convention. Of course, if they lost the game, well, everything else was just crap.

Bear Bryant later admitted the Aggies were "about five touchdowns better, talent-wise."

They had come a long way from Junction.

Two weeks following the NCAA meeting, the Aggies outlasted a Texas team that won once all year and not at all in the SWC. The Darrell Royal era would begin the following season.

Final score: A&M 34, Texas 21. And of course, John David played his customary bulldogging role.

"It sounds horrible now," John David says, "but I had them shoot my foot with Novocain, and I never felt any pain during the game. I would have played without it if they hadn't let me take the shot, but it made things easier."

When reporters asked the jubilant Crow how it felt to break the Longhorn hex in Austin, he replied, "It was no jinx. There just hasn't been an Aggie team like the Fighting Aggies of '56."

You know what? He wasn't exaggerating at all.

The players threw Bear Bryant in the showers.

"Most of us who had been on the field all day were

too tired to help out," John David says. "I was in on it, but I think Coach Bryant's shower was a bigger thrill for the Junction Boys playing their last game. In two years, they had gone from 1-9 to an undefeated season. That was worth celebrating."

A couple of the Junction Boys, Dennis Goehring and Jack Pardee, were all-Americans, along with Charlie Krueger.

As an inside linebacker, Pardee attacked runners like Jackie Gleason rummaging through the refrigerator for one more hot dog. Pardee later said of the Junction Boys, "We built something together instead of inheriting it or having somebody give it to us. For that, we will always be grateful to Coach Bryant."

The Aggies' stature had grown, all over campus and all over Texas. The Junction Boys had completed their duty.

Meanwhile, neighbors had taken Johnny to visit parents in Fort Worth, allowing Carolyn and John David to stay overnight at an Austin hotel – as they painted the town maroon, so to speak, in celebration of the 9-0-1 season.

When they returned to the hotel from partying, John David could not get out of the car. The pain was back in his foot at an excruciating level. Carolyn had to retrieve a chair from the room so he could use it as a crutch.

Not only was a bone already chipped, playing had further torn up the inside of the foot. They had enough money for aspirins; and, when the Crows reached Fort Worth, their friends had been kind enough to buy a pair of crutches.

"I later ended up having surgery in Houston to re-

move some chips," John David says. "It wasn't too pleasant at the time, but my reward for playing that game is that it allowed me to miss all of spring training."

John David rushed for 561 yards on 101 carries as a junior, a 5.6 average per carry. He was the leading receiver, with six catches for 117 yards. He completed two of seven passes for 12 yards. And he led the conference in points scored with 60 – eight touchdowns on the ground, two by air.

Once again, he may have been even better on defense. He wasn't just a quick and physical safety, he was smart, too.

John David had become perhaps the most dynamic force in perhaps the most dynamic conference in the country.

Bobby Joe Conrad, his road-game roommate for four years at A&M and a great talent himself, says, "John David had a big hand in every game. He had a great presence. And believe me, whoever tackled him felt it."

"He probably had a better junior year than he did a senior year," Pardee says. "He was one of the rare quality players anywhere in the country – a big guy with real good speed. And if he had been allowed to spend all his time on defense, he probably would have been great without ever carrying the football."

But two years of probation had deprived the Junction Boys as well as the class known as The Team of Tomorrow of two major bowl games, where their national reputation might have been further enhanced.

Even without much television.

The five Aggie seniors on offense who led A&M to No. 1: John David (44), Richard Gay (30), Bobby Lockett (84), Ken Beck (72) and Bobby Marks (88).

CHAPTER EIGHT

Finally, No. 1

Early in the fall of 1957, a reporter asked Bear Bryant about John David's chances of making all-America.

Bryant looked at the guy as if he had a piece of dried Juicy Fruit stuck up a nostril and replied, "He's gonna pick the team."

The Junction Boys and all those reliable minutes on both sides of the football were gone. The freshman class known as the Team of Tomorrow had become the Team of Now, as well as inheritors of the 10-game undefeated streak.

But, the two recruiting classes following John David's lacked enough snap, crackle and pop to provide sufficient depth. The NCAA's two-year probation, which could not have been more untimely, had been lifted, but quality prospects had chosen to go elsewhere because of it.

Immediately following the probation, Bryant informed his assistant coaches and alumni they best not even give a recruiter's mama a handkerchief if she sneezed. The Aggies no doubt lost some of their enthusiasm for recruiting.

Society continued to change, as well. Some teenage boys turned their attention from war heroes and gallant cowboys to Elvis Presley and James Dean. Dean was the ultimate rebel without a cause. He had died in a 1955 car crash, but his legend was just getting kick-started.

Elvis was only six months older than John David. Presley's first chart buster, *Heartbreak Hotel*, and movie, *Love Me Tender*, were both released in 1956. Over the next two years, he dominated Billboard's hit list with 10 No. 1 singles. Radios blared with the rock 'n roll of

Chuck Berry, Sam Cooke, Fats Domino, Buddy Holly, Ricky Nelson, Little Richard and on and on.

"Carolyn and I and a few others were waiting for an elevator at the Shamrock Hilton in Houston after the Rice game one year when the doors opened and there was Elvis," John David says. "He was just starting to get popular. He had all that hair, and I didn't like that. The girls did. Before he got off the elevator and we got on, he looked right at Carolyn, and I think if he'd got back on, I probably would have hit him."

Cadets don't wear ducktails. As hard as Bryant's staff hustled, they had a hard time recruiting this new breed to an all-male school in the middle of a prairie.

Beginning in 1958, the Aggies would suffer through nine consecutive losing seasons – the streak not ending until one of the Junction Boys, Gene Stallings, coached them to the 1967 Southwest Conference championship, as well as a victory over Alabama and his old coach, Bear Bryant, in the Cotton Bowl Classic.

The 1957 Aggies would close out arguably the most remarkable, legendary four-year span in school history.

But they were thinner than taffy. Bryant relied almost exclusively on 15 players for 11 physically demanding Saturdays. The talent level dramatically dropped off after those 15. Most starters averaged at least 50 of the 60 playing minutes per game.

Kenneth Hall had packed his bags following the bloody Baylor

game in '56. Many of those 100-plus players that raced endlessly from the tunnel for their freshman opener had gone on to run endlessly into the night, giving up their scholarships rather than enduring Bear Bryant's demanding workouts.

Only 12 of them completed their senior year of eligibility at A&M.

"We missed that Junction mentality," John David says. "We missed Goehring's toughness. Richard Gay and John Gilbert did a good job as the inside linebackers, but the guys they replaced, Pardee and Lloyd Hale, were truly great players. We were far too thin by major college standards."

Years later, Bryant said Gay would have been an all-American if he had moved him from fullback to center. Bear had a serious hankering to make the switch, which would have allowed him to put John David at fullback ("So that we could have run the option both ways," Bryant explained). He would have also shifted Roddy Osborne from quarterback to halfback, installed Loyd Taylor at the other halfback and used Jim Wright and Charlie Milstead at quarterback.

But Pardee, who began his long, notable pro career that season as a linebacker for the Los Angeles Rams, isn't so sure Bryant would have ever made the move.

"Coach Bryant was emphatic about playing his fullback at inside linebacker on defense and his halfbacks in the defensive backfield," Pardee says. "John David may have been the best combination running back/safety in the country as a junior. It would have been awfully tough to switch someone that good at two positions to two other positions, regardless of the reasons."

Bryant also later admitted that if he hadn't run off Ken Hall, the Aggies would have won the national championship in 1957.

They came close anyway.

But for John David, his final season at Aggieland began with more whimper than boom. He injured a knee early in the opener, a windy and rainy 21-13 victory over

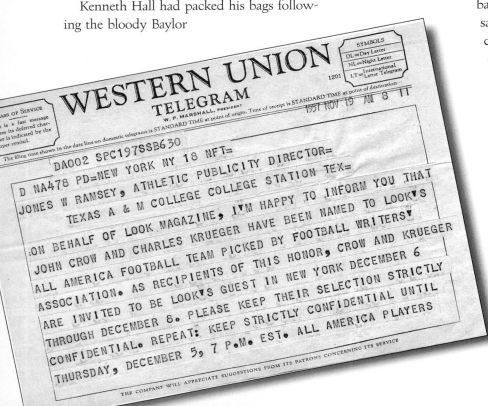

Maryland, in Dallas' Cotton Bowl. The win gave Paul Bryant a taste of revenge over the first school to hire him, then let him go.

Neither John David nor Loyd Taylor even suited out for the second game, a 21-0 victory over Texas Tech; and, Crow was used sparingly in a 28-6 whipping of Missouri.

In effect, his senior season began at the Kyle Field season opener against Houston. The Cougars had been the lone team to so much as tie the Aggies a year earlier, when Bryant passed up a field goal from the UH one-yard line with seconds to go. That Houston blemish prevented the Aggies' undefeated streak of 13 games from being a consecutive-game winning streak, which was at 10 nonetheless.

John David punched across two touchdowns against Houston, busted open holes, and was a perfect decoy for Osborne, who scampered for 116 yards on 21 carries and the other two touchdowns in a 28-6 victory.

Bear's Aggies were making serious national waves, entering conference play with a 4-0 record, having outscored the opposition, 98-25.

In the SWC opener, the Aggies held off rugged TCU, 7-0. But it wasn't easy. Osborne tossed a short touchdown pass to Bobby Marks only six minutes into the game, and it would not have been the day's only score except a defense spearheaded by Crow, tackle Ken Beck and linebacker Richard Gay stalled four TCU drives: one at the A&M five, two at the six and another at the 11.

A&M's record climbed to 6-0, the undefeated streak to 16 games and the winning streak to 12 with another shutout, this one 14-0 against old nemesis Baylor. John David's six-yard touchdown run in the fourth quarter iced it.

In the last week of October, for the first time since John Kimbrough led the '39 squad to the national title, The Associated Press and UPI polls tabbed Texas A&M No. 1 in the land.

The season would end only a month later, in the traditional Thanksgiving Day game against Texas. The Aggies had not lost since the Texas game closed out John David's sophomore season in 1955.

If those 15 worn-down players could just hang on ... Bear's defense must have made his heart swell. In six

games, the Aggies had given up 25 points. John David was busier than a World Book encyclopedia salesman – running tough, blocking tough, kicking, crashing into runners, returning punts, batting away passes and making interceptions (his five led the team).

"Just having him on your side was one helluva plus, and that was before the game started," says Krueger, who repeated as an all-America tackle. "Defensively, John was fast enough to get where he needed to be and strong enough to physically pound them. In most all cases on either side of the ball, John David did not take the pounding. He gave it."

"I can tell you this: He helped my performance as a blocker, because I knew if I didn't get my guy moving, Crow was gonna be blowing up through there with the ball, running over both of us. It sounds like a joke, but it really was an intimidating factor."

Crow and Krueger were co-captains in 1957, and Bear was fond of both. Bryant would walk up to Crow after he'd flattened a teammate in goal-line practice and say for all to hear, "John David, I guess you better go on in before you hurt somebody."

John David returned the admiration – twofold. Even his senior year, while those close to A&M football discussed whether he might be the greatest Aggie of all time, John David remained frighteningly in awe of the big, gruff coach he had grown to respect like a second father.

"I'd see him coming toward me on campus, and I'd walk across the street or change directions," John David says. "I wasn't really afraid or intimidated, I just didn't want to have to make small talk with him ... Well, maybe I was a little intimidated."

Bum Phillips, an assistant coach that year, walked out of Bear's office one day and found John David shuffling around near the door.

"What do you need, John?" Bum asked.

"Just wanted to see The Man," John David said.

"Well, there's nobody in there with him. Why don't you just go on in?"

"Oh, I'll just wait," John David said, leaning against the wall.

A mere 40 years later, John David recalls, "I stood out there a long time. Every time I peeked my head inside,

The 1957 Aggies were undefeated and ranked No. 1 in the country after eight games, but lost the final three games by a total of six points, including a 3-0 loss to Tennessee in the Gator Bowl.

he looked busy. I was a kid then, and I wasn't about to bother him. Nobody bothered him."

George Blanda, the long-time pro quarterback and kicker who played for Bear at Kentucky, once proclaimed, "Every time Coach Bryant walks into a room I'm in, it makes me want to stand up and applaud."

"He never had to ask for your attention," Bum Phillips stated in Bryant's autobiography, *Bear*, "because he already had it."

"Everybody was shy around Bryant," Krueger says. "His own assistants were afraid of him, maybe even more than the players. I mean, we were just playing; but they had their livelihoods on the line."

Bear's reputation was spreading. The typical sports fan of the time could probably name a half-dozen college football coaches in the country, and Bryant was usually one of them.

If Bear had not won, nobody would have cared. But overnight, he had turned Kentucky first and then Texas A&M into national powers. And the way he won – the way he and his teams intimidated almost everyone in the

process – only enhanced his fame.

"Because we were the co-captains," Krueger says, "when there'd be a tough call to make, Crow would turn to me and say, 'What do you think?' And I'd tell him and we'd do it. It didn't dawn on me until later that John David figured if a mistake was gonna be made, he'd rather Coach Bryant jump on me than him."

Not that John David was the shy type on the field.

"Oh, when things got real tight," Krueger says, "Crow might say a few words to everybody, but I was real quiet. If I had a mouthful of rocks, I wouldn't open up."

Still the warmest relationship continued to be between Bryant's wife, Mary Harmon, and Carolyn.

And Johnny.

"Johnny was 2 years old, and a real joy," John David says. "I'd take him to the training room and we'd pass him around like a football. On Sunday afternoons and during the off-season, he'd go with me and run around the track.

"Mrs. Bryant just loved him. The real closeness was always more between Mrs. Bryant and Carolyn and Johnny than me and Coach Bryant. We were never real chummy; I just had a powerful respect for him."

In November, seven games into the 10-game regular season, the Aggies' first defense of the No. 1 ranking came in a most troublesome spot – Fayetteville, Arkansas.

For visitors indulging in sport against the beloved Razorbacks, The Hills of Arkansas have never been alive with the sound of music. Some 60,000 "Sooey Pig" screamers filled the air with their screeching anthem, cheering for the home boys to puncture A&M's No. 1 ranking as if it were a bad tire.

In the Southwest Conference, the Razorbacks were the ambassadors of the lone state outside the Lone Star state. Six other SWC teams represented schools, student bodies and alumni. The Razorbacks performed for an entire state. Not even the No. 1 team in the country scared them when the game was in The Hills.

Bryant knew that. He had already flashed back to the cheerful bus ride his players took on their way to the stadium two years earlier in Arkansas. On that ride, he had stopped the bus and called down John David for laughing out loud – and the Aggies and Hogs had tied that day.

This time, the day before the game, Bear announced, "John David owes a game to the team because he wasn't ready to play the last time we came here."

John David just looked at him sheepishly.

For the first time all year, an Aggie opponent scored first. After failing on the conversion, the Hogs were sitting sassy at 6-0.

The Aggies eventually retaliated with a 74-yard drive that culminated with John David skirting around right end from 12 yards out. Loyd Taylor booted the go-ahead point, the 18th consecutive conversion in 18 Aggie attempts – to date.

The Aggies clawed and scratched and made that margin stand up, still leading 7-6 with a mere 1:20 remaining. And, they had the ball on the Arkansas 12.

Bear sent in a sub just to remind quarterback Roddy Osborne to run the ball and the clock. Osborne was a gutsy winner with so-so skills. He was not hotly pursued by recruiters following his senior year at Gainesville High. He played fullback as a sophomore. A teammate

once said, "He's the only quarterback I know who can miss a handoff to the fullback and gain 13 yards."

Osborne had every intention of following Bryant's orders. He called for an option with Crow split out at flanker, but all Osborne planned to do was sprint around end, stay in-bounds, and watch the seconds tick away.

He faked a hand-off, turned, and found an Arkansas tackle preparing to wrap him up. He glanced into the end zone and spotted John David wide open at the goal line. Perhaps reflexively, Osborne threw the ball.

And now, all of a sudden, the national ranking and SWC title and long streaks were up in the air.

The ball had not traveled halfway to its intended receiver when Donny Horton, a sprinter, zipped in front of John David, intercepted and took off. The only player with a prayer of catching Horton was Osborne, one of the slower backs on the Aggie team.

Horton fled 64 yards, but Roddy Osborne pulled him down at the 27. Bear Bryant must have wet his pants twice – once when he saw Osborne put the ball in the air, and again when Osborne somehow ran down the speedster.

Bryant later explained, "Horton was just running for a touchdown. Osborne was running for his life."

Arkansas still had time, though – until John David saved the day with two amazing plays. Following a Hog reception in the open field, Crow dropped the receiver at the 15, saving an otherwise certain touchdown.

Arkansas quarterback George Walker failed on a pass into the end zone, then tried to catch the Aggies napping with the same play – and only five seconds remaining.

Walker spotted an open receiver and fired the ball toward the end zone. John David sprang that direction, thinking, "Oh, me, here it comes."

Just as the ball arrived in the receiver's hands for the winning score, Crow smacked him and popped the ball into the air.

As the ball came down again, John David somehow twisted to make the grab, then ran 14 yards to secure the 7-6 victory.

Bryant later called John David's game-savers "two of the greatest defensive plays I've ever seen in my life."

John David addresses a banquet crowd while new Texas coach Darrell Royal listens.

John David answered a few questions, then apologized to reporters, "I'm so sore right now I can't think."

Besides saving the game twice in the closing seconds, he had rushed for 115 yards on 13 carries and scored the lone touchdown.

The state of Arkansas was in shock. The Aggies, also perhaps shocked, returned to Texas 7-0 and still No. 1.

These were exciting times in Bryan/College Station, and for the farmers in the surrounding areas.

Leon Hale of The Houston Post, a city-side columnist with a gift for capturing small-town America, wrote this of Bryan/College Station the week following the Arkansas game:

"If indeed there is anything else to talk about, nobody is bothering to talk about it ... If the Brazos River suddenly flowed molten gold, it would have been a secondary development."

Most of the 5,000 cadets who greeted Bear Bryant at the airport upon his arrival were gone, but only in miles. Like so many other alumni, they returned for home games at Kyle Field, and Rice Stadium in Houston, and the Cotton Bowl in Dallas – all homes to the Aggies.

Those 5,000 had been there, like the Junction Boys,

from the beginning. This No. 1 rating was theirs, too.

Texas A&M was not a university yet. Dennis Goehring hadn't even opened his bank yet. Arkansas, Rice, Southern Methodist, Texas Christian and almost every opponent the Aggies faced – those were universities, including the one in Austin.

A&M was primarily an agricultural college, and most young men who went there could milk a cow, whether they owned one at the time or not. Oh, they could be a little rowdy and prankish at times, but there wasn't much real meanness in them. They were male, for the most part white and wide-eyed; and, quite frankly, they were probably having more fun than the Little Rascals. Whether the rest of the state knew it or not.

The growth spurt would not begin for another six years, when in 1963 A&M opened its doors to women. Today, enrollment is almost ten times the number of students who attended Bear Bryant's manly striptease at the Grove and bellowed loudly at the words "national championship," as if it might actually be in the cards.

Three more victories would do it.

Following the one in Fayetteville, Bear said, "We must have played a great game or we couldn't have run up the score on 'em like that."

But deep down, he knew his players were weary. The deeper the Aggies went into the season, the tougher it became for them to stay fresh against opponents using twice the players.

A date with SMU back home at Kyle followed Arkansas, and the Mustangs battled A&M to a 6-6 draw for a half. But John David snuffed out two serious threats with interceptions against SMU's dandy quarterback, Don Meredith, and in the third quarter, the Aggies put together a 14-play, 65-yard winning march. John David, who sometimes was not handed the ball 10 times in a game, carried nine times on the drive for 49 yards, including the two-yard TD.

The Aggies went on to whip SMU, 19-6, extending the unbeaten streak to 18, the win streak to 14, and the record to 8-0. About the only real downer came when Loyd Taylor missed an extra point, the Aggies' first failed conversion all year.

With every player keying on him, John David rushed

for 89 yards, returned punts and a kickoff for 64 yards, kicked an extra point, scored a touchdown, stole a sure touchdown with one of his two interceptions, and blocked like an ice house on wheels.

Bill Rives, sports editor of The Dallas Morning News, called Crow "a superman in shoulder pads." Writers were comparing his all-around ability to that of SMU's Doak Walker, the conference's last Heisman Trophy winner in 1948.

Charles Burton in The Dallas Morning News wrote, "John Crow is an all-America football player and three times as good as he was last season, when he merely was a sensation."

The Aggies were within two wins of a perfect regular season and a national championship: one in Houston against Rice, and the Thanksgiving finale at Kyle Field against Darrell Royal's first Texas squad.

A win or even a tie against Rice would clinch the conference title because the Owls had already lost once, and they were closer to the Aggies than anybody else.

In just three years, it appeared ol' Bear had lapped the field.

The *Time* magazine of Nov. 25, 1957, began a sports brief: THE OWLS & THE CROW.

It hardly seemed a happy Homecoming Day for the Rice Institute Owls. Texas A&M was in town, and the awesome Aggies were flaunting a 14-game winning streak, ranking No. 1 in the nation and riding roughshod toward the Cotton Bowl on the broad shoulders of John David Crow, everybody's All-American and the hardest-running halfback in college football. Short of calling on some friendly farmer to shoot down Crow, the Owls figured to be pecked to pieces.

But those wise birds were tougher than they looked.

The national championship simply was not in the cards for the Aggies, after all.

A standing room only crowd of 72,000 packed Rice Stadium. Most had read or heard about an article by Jack Gallagher in The Houston Post that morning. The story suggested rumors coming out of Alabama may have some substance: Bear Bryant might be returning to his alma mater.

Bear said the rumors were as stale as last week's pie,

and that he had a football game to play. But the story had to be a distraction.

Jess Neely's Owls were good enough to be ranked 20th nationally, thanks among others to the superb quarterbacking duo of King Hill and Frank Ryan (the substitution rule had changed, as it often did in those days, allowing free subbing at QB but nowhere else).

Hill picked off a Charlie Milstead pass deep in Rice territory in the first quarter, and Ryan led Rice on a 79-yard drive before Hill sneaked in from one yard out. Hill's extra point put the Aggies in a 7-0 hole.

Back came A&M behind Osborne, who eventually wiggled down to the Owl 2 on a critical fourth-and-two call from the six. It took him three more tries to crack the end zone, and he did on the first play of the final quarter.

But Loyd Taylor's extra-point attempt wobbled wide right, leaving the Aggies down by a point with 14:58 still showing.

Later, the Aggies pulled within field-goal range again. Maybe Bear grew flustered that Taylor had missed two conversions in two weeks and didn't want to lose a national title on an errant foot. The Owls stopped them again.

The Aggies also coughed up six fumbles on a day when King Hill's punts were giving them headaches anyway. Hill kicked out of bounds at the Aggie one-yard line with only four minutes remaining and Rice still ahead, 7-6.

Incredibly, a few plays later John David gave the Aggies one last ray of hope. He broke loose for 21 yards and had a long, open field ahead when he momentarily stumbled, allowing Hill to make up ground more quickly.

"King Hill was the only player who could have caught me when I broke into the clear," John David says. "But, as I recall, instead of squaring up on him where I could have cut either way, I let him use the sidelines to hem me in."

It ended, 7-6. A&M's three-week reign as No. 1 was over. The Aggies have not been No. 1 in the country since.

The undefeated streak had been halted – one shy of the 19-game string put together by that last great bunch of Aggies in the late 1930's and early 40's.

Bear said he should have gone for the field goal, and

accepted additional blame by philosophizing: "Just mark it down to the difference in coaching and preparation."

The revved-up Owls went on to represent the SWC in the Cotton Bowl, for the last time.

Stunned and downhearted, with rumors of Bryant's imminent departure for Alabama still circling the campus, the Aggies had to wait 12 days for the Thanksgiving Day scuffle against Texas.

By kickoff, the Aggies knew they still had a slim chance of winning the conference – but only if Rice lost to Baylor two days after Thanksgiving on the last weekend of the regular season. Baylor had not won an SWC game all year.

However, there was some good news. During Thanksgiving week, the Sugar Bowl committee let it leak out that if Rice did beat Baylor as expected, New Orleans would be most pleased to welcome the A&M/UT winner to its big bash.

That was before the Longhorns ripped the insides out of the Aggies with a 9-7 victory at Kyle Field.

Texas scored early and hung on in a hard-fought game completely controlled by the defenses and punting games. UT's Bobby Lackey, a quarterback who could not throw a spiral but won with finesse, totaled a mere 36 yards running and passing. But his 38-yard field goal in the third quarter clinched it, propelling the 5-4-1 Longhorns into the Sugar Bowl.

Lackey's clutch boot sailed close enough to one of the uprights that Bryant wasn't certain. The ball flopped right into the arms of Aggie freshman manager Frank Hernandez, assigned to retrieve the ball beyond the end zone on field goal efforts.

When Hernandez returned to the Aggie sidelines, Bryant asked, "Was that kick good?"

"Yes, Coach, it sure was," Hernandez said.

Bryant hurled his baseball cap to the ground (his famous houndstooth hat would not become a part of his daily attire until Alabama) and kicked it.

Afterward, he told reporters, "Texas should have beaten us worse than they did, and would have if Crow had not knocked down a lot of passes."

Crow carried 21 times for 64 yards, completed a pass and caught one that stretched 57 yards to the 10 by the

John David traveled to New York City to appear with the 1957 all-America team on the Ed Sullivan show.

time he was finally brought down. He scored three plays later from the one. He knocked down countless passes and seemed to be in on every other tackle.

Mickey Herskowitz, now a columnist with The Houston Chronicle, says, "There's this portrait of John David I still have in my memory, as clear as ever. He's just been tackled and he's trying to get up after the long pass play. He's completely spent but slowly pulling himself up, the portrait of a player who had given every ounce in him."

In less than three weeks, A&M went from first in the nation to third in the conference.

"Dropping that far that fast is unquestionably the biggest disappointment in my football career," John David says.

Charlie Krueger knows the feeling: "It was a knocker, especially coming at the end of our senior years when we couldn't do anything about it."

Directly following the loss to Texas, Bryant came close to admitting the Alabama rumors might be a little more than rumor.

"Say you were out playing as a kid and heard your mama call," he explained to the shoulder-to-shoulder reporters jostling for elbow room in his little office. "If you thought she wanted you to do the chores, you might not answer. But if you thought she needed you, you'd be there in a hurry."

Two days later, Bryant accepted the Alabama job.

John David, King Hill of Rice (middle) and Charlie Krueger (right) pose at LaGuardia Airport to kick off the gathering of Look's 1957 all-America team in New York City.

John David says he has no clear memory of Bryant announcing his departure to the players.

"It would have mattered a good deal more to guys like Charlie Milstead who were coming back," Crow says. "I was just about finished at A&M anyway."

Krueger says Bryant did try explaining his decision to the team at least once.

"Every day we had a short meeting after lunch, before going to classes," Krueger recalls. "He brought us into a meeting room in the A&M mess hall and started

telling us, but he choked up."

Bear stepped out of the room, and a couple of his assistants completed his message.

Bryant's four years at Texas A&M perfectly coincided with those of John David. In Crow's three varsity years, the Aggies lost the first and last games of his sophomore season and not again until the late skid. The Team of Tomorrow went 24-2-2 before the late fade.

When word came that the Gator Bowl wanted the Aggies and Tennessee to face off in Jacksonville, Fla., that

John David joins in signing several boxes of footballs to be given to children in local New York City hospitals.

December 27, Bryant knew the player reaction might be a might on the tepid side, after losing the streaks and the conference and the Cotton and Sugar invites.

So he ordered his co-captains to let the team vote on it.

Crow and Krueger returned to his office a bit later. Charlie stood by sheepishly as John David said, "Coach, we voted not to go."

There came a long pause – because nobody else in the room talked if it might be Bear's turn – and then Bryant said, "Well, you go back in there and get another vote, because I've already accepted."

Needless to say, the 8-2 Aggies, No. 9-ranked in the nation, had one more game to play, in Florida in a month.

And what a strange month December 1957, would be for those passionate Aggies. An era was ending so suddenly, with a more or less meaningless bowl game following two years of probation that prevented them

from attending bigger bowls.

But also that month, all the various all-America teams would be announced, all including the name John David Crow. The National Football League would hold its draft, and the Chicago Cardinals would use the first two picks to snatch up John David with one and King Hill of Rice with the other.

And the Heisman Trophy would be awarded – to John David Crow. That meant going to New York City to accept the award as college football's greatest player of 1957.

And Carolyn would be there to see it. So would Harry and Velma Crow, parents so proud that for the first time in John David's life, he actually saw tears in his dad's eye.

Harry's boy – and Bear's, too – would be standing at a podium, looking out at more than 1,000 people, saying thank you to them as they smiled and applauded and said thank you back.

CHAPTER NINE

The Heisman

J ohn David, Carolyn and Johnny were in Springhill for the semester break in December 1957, when Velma picked up a ringing phone and said hello back to Dr. M.T. Harrington, the president of Texas A&M. John David returned to the house after visiting around town, and Velma said, "Dr. Harrington called to say you've won the Heisman Memorial Trophy."

She might have received a stronger reaction had she told him the latest soda fountain flavors at Tennyson's. John David did not begin to grasp the relevance until his mother added, "It must be a big thing because they're going to fly Carolyn, your daddy and me to New York for the ceremonies."

John David was already dizzy from the changes suddenly impacting his life and his family. The Chicago Cardinals, the worst team in the National Football League, had announced they would use their first two overall picks in the draft that month on John David and King Hill of Rice.

John David was going to be paid a decent salary to continue to do what he loved most.

How do you top that one?

He already knew he'd be flying to New York to appear on the Ed Sullivan and Bob Hope television shows with the rest of that year's first-team all-America honorees.

How do you top that one either?

He would just stay in New York a couple more days for this Heisman thing, and not only would his parents and Carolyn be joining him, Coach Elmer was going, too.

"We drove out to the paper mill where dad was working," John David recalls, "and when I saw him getting teary-eyed, I realized the Heisman might be a bigger deal than I thought. It was the first time in my life I ever saw my daddy with tears in his eyes."

John David's 1,183 points marked the fifth-highest Heisman vote total in the 23-year history of the award. The margin of victory – almost 500 points over Iowa tackle Alex Karras (693 points) – illustrates the impact John David's defense and blocking and all-around game had on voters.

Michigan State halfback Walt Kowalczyk (630) and Kentucky tackle Lou Michaels (330) followed Karras.

The sculpture is of a running back hugging a football to his chest with his left hand while warding off an imaginary tackler with a right-hand stiff-arm.

Though the Modern Museum of Art or the Guggenheim may not display the Heisman Memorial Trophy, it is the Rodin of college football.

John David won almost every award handed out his senior year: the Walter Camp Award, the Today Award, the Harley Award, the H.C. Miller Award, the Hula Bowl Trophy, The Houston Post Trophy, the Houston A&M Award, *Sport* Magazine's College Football Player of the Year Award, NCAA first-team all-America, *Look* Magazine All-America (announced live on the Bob Hope Show), the Kentucky Colonel Certificate, the Movietone News All-America team (live on Ed Sullivan), and at least 10 others.

"When people ask me what awards and honors I got in college, I just tell them the Heisman," John David says. "If you've got it, what more do you need to say?"

His original 1957 Heisman sits high on a shelf in the den of the Crows' house and is the room's only noticeable reminder that John David ever played football. A

John David and Carolyn enjoyed several nights out on the town while in New York City.

replica Heisman is the star attraction of a trophy case on the Texas A&M campus at the John J. Koldus Building and in the Bryant Museum on the campus of the University of Alabama in Tuscaloosa, Ala.

But John David had always been so immersed in the team-first concept, to now suddenly be singled out – not only among the competition but his own teammates, well, that was unnerving. The live TV appearances had been fun, with John David lined up right there on stage with the other all-Americas.

"A rrrrrreally big shew," as Ed Sullivan promised.

But this Heisman Trophy was so very different.

The 1957 Texas A&M media guide does not include thumbnail sketches or brief bios of the players on the Aggie football team.

Almost one-third of its 43 pages is a records section. Seven pages detail that year's opponents, a couple more list notable Southwest Conference statistics, and there are single pages on the coaching staff, the team roster, travel plans, the 12th Man legend, the school's history, future schedules, Kyle Field info and other what-nots.

By today's standards, omission of the individual

the D.A.C. journal

JANUARY 1958

achievements of star players would appear akin to handing an Italian chef a new pizza recipe without furnishing the quantity for each ingredient.

That year's co-captains, John David Crow and Charlie Krueger, adorn the cover, accompanied by the headline "A&M's All-America candidates," but that's about the extent of the ballyhoo.

There was no clever season-long campaign for John David as a Heisman candidate. Jones Ramsey, A&M's jovial sports information director, ranked among the greats in his field, but nobody in those days was dreaming up clever slogans or releasing glossy material that might give their player an edge over other candidates.

Football played right was a team sport, especially under Paul Bryant.

And yet, during the course of the 1957 season, two unlikely "campaign managers" influenced that year's voting for college football's premier player.

One was a reporter, Mickey Herskowitz, just trying to do a thorough, objective job for The Houston Post. The other was Bear Bryant, just telling the truth in the rawest of fashions.

Herskowitz was 19 years old and a freshman at the University of Houston when, in 1954, Bryant's arrival in College Station prompted Post sports editor Clark Nealon to make Herskowitz the first Aggies beat writer in the state.

"Not even the high school beat man wanted the job," says Herskowitz, who went on to become one of the premier sports chroniclers in the country. "I made the drive from Houston to College Station so many times I was handed four speeding tickets in one month. Nealon said if I got another one, he was going to enter me in the Indianapolis 500."

No one intentionally ran John David for the Heisman, but Herskowitz was almost always on hand when Bryant grunted out another compliment. And when Bear said something nice about one of his players, it most certainly was news.

Take the way he referred to his other players by their last names. When he started saying "John David" instead of Crow, everybody noticed. Players, opponents, writers. The shift was subtle only if one

Harry and Velma Crow join their son, John David, in celebrating his Heisman Trophy.

"The good Lord, a group of fine boys – and Old Crow."

When John David walked off the field for his final college game, the 9-7 loss to Texas, Bear declared, "John David is the greatest athlete who ever lived, for my money."

And when Herskowitz asked him if Crow merited the honor as college football's player of the year?

Bryant's comment ran all over the country:

"If he doesn't win the Heisman, they ought to stop giving it."

And yet, Bear was not leading off press conferences with a "vote-for-my-boy" song-and-dance. He didn't go car to car in the media parking lot attaching "Vote John David" fliers to windshields.

A little here and there went a very long way.

"Around the players," Bobby Joe Conrad says, "Coach Bryant always kept the team aspect going. He might have pushed John David with the media on occasion, but nobody in College Station was paying much attention because there wasn't a local daily paper or any local television coverage. Nobody sat around talking about the Heisman."

The Heisman was largely an Eastern award created and presented by the Downtown Athletic Club of New York. It originally was intended to honor the best player east of the Mississippi River, but since the year following its inception in 1935 the Heisman has gone to the country's best college player, as determined by a vote of select media members and previous winners.

A player in the East, or with Notre Dame or one of

assumed Bryant ever said anything subtle. In actuality, Bryant was shouting for the college football world to hear, "I like this kid."

Every so often, Bryant would serve up a classic one-liner and Herskowitz would circulate it. First, the quote ran in The Houston Post, and then practically every notes columnist in the country would lift it for their own publications.

Late in the '57 season, Herskowitz asked Bryant to explain how a running back about to finish with a little more than 500 yards rushing (562), fourth in his own conference, might even be considered as a Heisman candidate.

Bear drawled, "That may be true, but if you count the folks he's run over you'll find he leads the nation in that category – people run over."

Following the 7-6 squeaker over Arkansas in The Hills, Bryant was asked the keys to the game. He answered,

John David was selected to play in the 1958 College All-Star Game.

the military academies, had an edge because the Eastern papers were more apt to cover their games. But the Southwest Conference had a rich heritage of producing tremendous talent like TCU quarterback Davey O'Brien, the fourth Heisman winner; TCU quarterback Sammy Baugh, a worthy candidate two years before O'Brien; TCU running back Jim Swink, deserving the year before John David's selection; SMU's do-everything running back Doak Walker, the 1948 Heisman winner; Texas quarterback Bobby Layne in the mid-1940's; and, of course, John Kimbrough of the Aggies (second in the 1940 voting to Michigan's Tom Harmon).

And yet, as Charlie Krueger says, "Down in the Southwest, we thought of the Heisman as an Eastern press

thing. We never gave it a thought."

Including John David.

"The Heisman was not even a part of my life until it was announced," he says. "I was already getting questionnaires and Western Union telegrams from pro football teams wanting to know about my military obligations and my interest in their organizations. Carolyn and I began to realize for the first time that I could probably play pro ball.

"Chicago had the two closest pro teams to College Station, so whoever was home that Sunday – the Bears or the Cardinals – we would get on television. But we never sat around and dreamed, 'This is what we're going to be doing next.' It just never dawned on us. And neither did the Heisman."

If the vote had been left up to boys playing sandlot football all over Texas, John David might have won more than one Heisman. He was very much in their minds, and so was his jersey number, 44.

As a youngster, R.C. Slocum played in neighborhood yards around his hometown, Orange, in Southeast Texas.

"We were all aware of that number," says Slocum, who grew up to become a head coach of some renown. "Somebody was always pretending to be John David. Radios and newspapers were our main sources of information, so listening to Kern Tips describe that Aggie team on the radio was very exciting to me and my friends."

Mike Jones, a sportswriter for The Fort Worth Star-Telegram, played eighth-grade football in the East Texas town of Kilgore the year after John David won the Heisman.

"We all envied Eugene McKenzie because he had No. 44 and wouldn't give it up no matter what the offer," Jones says. "I didn't like him anyway because he had a '55 Chevy Belaire, pink and gray. Guess which one of us dated the cheerleaders."

Before Aggie home games, freshman manager Frank

Hernandez was among a small group that slipped outside the stadium to hock the players' season tickets. They discovered that if John David signed ALL the tickets, they could bring back a bigger haul.

Hernandez, who went on to become the first Hispanic judge in Dallas County history, recalls, "Some Aggie alumnus would ask me how much for the tickets, and I'd say, 'Forty dollars each,' which was very high then. He'd say, 'Forty dollars!' I'd hold out the tickets and show where John David had signed them and say, 'These are John David's tickets, and if I don't get forty each, he's gonna get mad at me.' Then the alumnus would go, 'Oh, OK,' and dig into his pockets. We called it our marketing scheme."

John David also autographed chin straps and let the managers give them to the children running onto Kyle Field following home games.

His older sister, Doris, was still living in Springhill at the time. She looks back on those days and says, "His notoriety was such a shock to all of us. We didn't realize it was actually happening. We would hear stuff about him and it was almost like they were talking about somebody else."

Carolyn and Coach Elmer took a bumpy flight from Easterwood Airport to Love Field in Dallas, where they met up with Velma and Harry Crow and lit out on a big Delta plane for the biggest city any of them could imagine. Velma and Harry had never been on a plane before. It was a thrill for all of them.

The day before the banquet, John David was introduced to the press at a luncheon jointly sponsored by the Downtown Athletic Club and the New York Football Writers Association.

Asked whether he had encountered any hardships as a married player, John David told a group of reporters, "When I was a little boy, I once overheard a grown-up say, 'A woman can make or break you.' Well, my wife made me ... I don't think many college football coaches are happy about having married players on their squads, but being married helped me. I wouldn't be here in New York waiting to be awarded the Heisman Trophy if it hadn't been for her. She kept my feet on the ground."

Dr. Harrington joined them the night before the Heis-

man banquet at a small gathering at the Downtown Athletic Club, which looked out onto the Statue of Liberty. The group proceeded to Toot's Shors, the legendary restaurant/bar in midtown Manhattan, for a few after-dinner cocktails.

Coach Bryant decided not to attend; he had to hit the recruiting trail for his new team, Alabama, before rejoining the Aggies for practices leading up to the Gator Bowl. But he also wanted this to be Elmer Smith's moment in the spotlight – a way of thanking his assistant for luring John David to A&M.

Then, on Dec. 11, 1957, more than 1,000 well-dressed football fans and Downtown Athletic Club members filled the banquet room, where John David was the guest of honor. Following the meal, they packed the Downtown A.C. gymnasium and awaited the magic moment. The Mutual Broadcasting System was also there, carrying the presentation live from coast to coast on the radio.

John David had never spoken to a crowd before.

He took his seat at the main table near the dais, next to the president of DAC.

The president asked John David what he was going to say.

"I don't really know," John David answered.

"Well, just get up there and say what you have to say and sit down," the president suggested.

When the time came, John David stepped to the podium as the 1,000 onlookers gave him a standing ovation.

"The No. 1 Person knows how much I thank Him," John David said into the microphone. "I'll be looking back on this occasion as long as I live, and I hope to set an example for other high school boys who will one day receive the support I have here tonight."

He paused and lightly slid his hand along the black and gold running back in his hands. And in that split second, he thought about the president's words: say what you have to say and sit down.

"It all seems like a dream," John David said. "And I want to sit down before I make a racket that might wake me."

He had done himself, his family, and Aggies everywhere proud.

Back in Texas, John David was besieged by a string of

post-Heisman interviews. During one, Harless Wade of The Dallas Morning News questioned him about his powerful, bulldozing runs.

John David replied, "I've read and heard that I'm a guy who likes to knock people down. I've been quoted as saying that I enjoy it, that I'm the bruiser type. Where in the world did this all start? Look, I'm human like everybody else, and humans don't like to go knocking humans down. Sure, I knock players down in a game, but that's football. Otherwise, I wouldn't be doing it."

For the Aggies, he'd only be doing it once more, in the Gator Bowl against Tennessee.

The Aggies were obviously in some disarray. Bryant's imminent departure to Alabama, the two-week slide from No. 1 in the nation to No. 3 in the conference, the end of the undefeated streak, all took their toll.

But Bear Bryant only knew one way to prepare his team, and John David Crow, Heisman winner, was about to be reminded.

"For practices," Hernandez, the manager, explains, "we had four different-colored jerseys. The starters wore maroon, the second team wore white, the third wore orange, and the fourth green. Everyday the managers were given a list that let us know what color jersey to hang in each locker.

"When John David returned from the Heisman ceremony, Coach Bryant had him down for a green jersey. John David put it on, but when he went outside he trotted over to be with the maroon team."

Bryant ordered Hernandez to run tell John David to join the green jerseys. When Hernandez carried the message, Crow looked at him and said, "I ain't gonna do it."

Hernandez ran back to Bryant and said, "Coach, he says that's not gonna happen."

Bear squinted and looked out over the field and said, "Oh, well. Go get him a maroon jersey. He probably deserves it."

In another practice that week, John David leveled a teammate on a run. Bryant ranted at one of his assistants, "I've told ya'll not to let John David hurt these people!"

On the next series, with John David on defense, a player scored. This time Bryant yelled out, "That's why you'll never be worth a damn! Cause you can't

take a compliment!"

Try as he might, Bryant could not get his team pumped up. Players began to grumble, questioning the severity of the practices.

John David finally went to Bryant's office and asked why the practices had to be so rough when he was leaving and many of them were, too.

"I've got to do things my way," Bryant said. "This is the only way I know how to get a football team ready to play."

John David said, "Yes, sir," and got up and left.

On December 27, Tennessee nudged the Aggies, 3-0, in one of the roughest defensive struggles in Gator Bowl history. Most of the game was played between the 30-yard lines, until late in the fourth quarter when the Vols took over at midfield and drove to the one before kicking the winning field goal.

The Aggies had lost their final three games by a total of six points.

Their three-year record with John David was 24-5-2. The Aggie defense had allowed seven or fewer points in 22 of their 31 games, including seven shutouts.

Forty years later, in August 1997, John David and Carolyn attended the ceremonies for the unveiling of the Paul Bryant U.S. postage stamp in Alabama. A fan approached John David and said, "I can still remember that unbelievable collision you had with Bobby Gordon in the Gator Bowl."

They had smashed head-on in a play that as much as any in his career typified John David's life-long approach to football.

"A lot of people think that was Johnny Majors, but he had graduated the year before," John David says. "I guess Bobby Gordon closed his eyes and I closed mine, and we had quite a collision. Every now and then somebody else will bring it up.

"The only reason I got up right away is because Gordon got up and went back to the Tennessee huddle. I was seeing stars when I noticed him just sort of collapsing, passing out."

To the very end, John David spent himself. And spent the other guy worse. Ultimately, that is his greatest legacy.

The world kept spinning faster. Springhill staged a

Springhill High coach Billy Baucum (left) and Bear Bryant join John David for "John Crow Day" in his hometown.

John David Crow Day, which included the Crows waving to old friends from the backseat of a convertible dragging Main Street. Coach Billy Baucum announced that John David's high school number, 35, had been retired since his senior year. Bear Bryant gave a nice little speech.

Then John David was in Honolulu for the Hula Bowl, playing for the College All-Americans against the highly favored Hawaii All-Stars, composed of seasoned NFL veterans.

Tobin Rote, who quarterbacked the Detroit Lions over the Cleveland Browns in the NFL Championship Game a week earlier, threw five touchdown passes. Joe Perry of the 49ers, one of the great backs of his day, rushed for 111 yards and scored four touchdowns.

The pros strolled to a 33-0 first quarter lead and 40-7

advantage at the half before being forced to hold on for a 53-34 victory.

John David? On 20 carries, he banged for 106 of his team's 166 rushing yards. He scored three touchdowns from three, 12 and three yards out.

The pros figured he was probably ready for the next level.

In May 1958, John David received a business degree from Texas A&M. He was also one of 34 Aggies selected to *Who's Who Among Students in American Colleges and Universities*.

"We always figured John David would take his degree and go to work for some big company in Houston or Dallas," Carolyn says.

When Carolyn and John David departed A&M, they had no reason to assume they would ever return to live in College Station. They pointed their hearts toward Chicago, where the pro draft was taking them.

But those first four years of marriage laid a strong foundation for a pair of teenagers from Springhill, Louisiana. John David says nine Aggie football players married while he was at A&M; he and Carolyn were the only ones to leave there together with a degree in hand.

In the foreword of the Aggieland '58 yearbook, the editors write, "We have not tried desperately to make this book beautiful ... for life at A&M is not always beautiful. Nor have we striven to portray the passing of but a single year in print and picture ... for A&M is not to be measured in terms of years.

"Our eternal watchword has been stark, utter simplicity, and after all, what is the true A&M but simplicity ... rugged, indelible.

"It is the tie that binds those who have gone before with those who are yet to come."

They could have been speaking of their greatest athlete, as well.

As R.C. Slocum, today's Aggie head coach, puts it, "John David Crow is the most recognizable name and athlete in the entire history of this university. Randy Matson (an Olympic shot-put gold-medal winner) would be second. Jarrin' John Kimbrough probably third."

CHAPTER TEN

Life as a Cardinal and a 49er

John David walked, and often limped, off the field on the losing end of the scoreboard nine times his first season with the Chicago Cardinals.

That's one more than his total number of defeats over the previous six years — as a junior and senior in high school, a freshman and three varsity seasons at A&M.

The Cardinals tied for last in the NFL's Eastern Division in 1958 with a 2-9-1 record in the days of the 12-game schedule. They were even more pathetic the next year, going 2-10 and finishing dead last.

The franchise moved to St. Louis in 1960, and struggled another three seasons before improving enough during John David's final two seasons there to go 9-5 in 1963 and 9-3-2 in 1964, when they finished within a tie of the first-place Cleveland Browns (10-3-1).

A trade sent the Crows packing to San Francisco for the final four seasons of John David's 11-year career. The 49ers displayed a remarkable consistency in going 27-25-4, somehow never doing worse than 6-6-2 or better than 7-6-1.

John David cuts back after seeing an opening in the Dallas Cowboys' defense during a game in Sportsman Park.

Had he not been such a sitting duck – keyed on by every defensive coordinator those years with the Cardinals – John David very likely would be a member of the NFL Hall of Fame.

One could put up a good argument on his behalf anyway.

"I think John David dominated more in the pros than he did in college," says Bobby Joe Conrad, Crow's road-game roommate first at A&M and again all seven years with the Cardinals. "He was always our go-to guy, and he pretty much carried the team."

Charlie Krueger, who also enjoyed a fruitful pro career that saw him and John David reunite in San Francisco, says, "Had John David gone to a winning team, someone like the New York Giants or a half-dozen others who really needed a strong running back, it would have changed his career altogether.

"He'd probably be in the Hall of Fame. I'll argue that with anybody. But, a lot of franchises lost because their owners and front offices didn't know what they were doing. You can take a great player and make him mediocre under the wrong structure. The Cardinals were one of those teams."

And this from Jack Pardee, who distinguished himself with the Los Angeles Rams: "John was about the only threat the Cardinals had, but nobody underestimated him because when you faced the Cardinals, that's what you were facing – John David.

"I got a lot better feel for his versatility and all-around abilities in the pros. But his best years were spent with a team that wasn't very good. If he had been at tailback in an I-formation or in one of today's offenses, he would have been even better. He had real good vision and a good change of direction."

John David loathes individual statistics, the way Bear Bryant did the forward pass.

But allow a comparison between John David's 11-year career (nine actually, he missed almost all of two seasons with injuries) and some of the premier backs of his day.

John David:

● Rushed for 1,252 more yards, caught twice as many passes (258-130), and scored 11 more touchdowns than Hall of Famer Paul Hornung;

● Accumulated 134 more career yards rushing and receiving, and scored 13 more TD's, than Hall of Famer Hugh McElhenny.

● Had 204 more career running/receiving yards than Hall of Famer Ollie Matson, and the same number of touchdowns (73).

● Scored 39 more pro touchdowns than Hall of Famer Doak Walker.

● Rushed for 243 more yards and scored 35 more TD's than Hall of Famer Marion Motley.

● Rushed for virtually the same amount of yards (seven more, actually), caught passes worth 2,396 more yards and scored 17 more touchdowns than the great Gayle Sayers.

Of his contemporaries, only Jimmy Brown, Jim Taylor and Joe Perry truly outdistanced Crow's all-around statistics, and they were fullbacks. Baltimore Hall of Famer Lenny Moore ran for only 211 more yards than John David's 4,963, while Giants Hall of Famer Frank Gifford, one of the most versatile backs in the game's history, amassed only 380 more running/receiving yards than John David's 8,662.

JOHN DAVID CROW
ST. LOUIS CARDINALS   HALFBACK

"I think John David dominated more in the pros than he did in college. He was always our go-to guy, and he pretty much carried the team."

Bobby Joe Conrad

Objections can easily be raised on behalf of the afore-mentioned Hall of Famers. Some will point out that Hornung, Gifford and Walker also kicked; Walker and Gifford played defensive back; and McElhenny and Matson returned punts and kickoffs.

But John David was a savage blocker. His blocking probably provided as much or more value to his team than a field-goal kicker, punter, or return man. He also threw 70 passes, nailing 33 for 759 yards, 23.0 yards per completion.

John David twice rushed for more than 1,000 yards in a 12-game season. No other Cardinal, including Ollie Matson, topped 1,000 once.

In 1960, John David led the NFL in average yards per carry with a 5.9 clip. That same year, he rushed for 203 yards on 24 carries against the Pittsburgh Steelers. No Cardinal before or since has eclipsed the 200-yard barrier in a game.

John David's 17 touchdowns in 12 games in 1962 is a club record that has not been eclipsed even in today's 16-game schedule. Four of those TD's came in one game.

John David was named All-Pro four times.

But Hornung was a winner surrounded by winners, as was Gifford and Taylor and Moore and other running back stars of the late 1950's and early 60's.

Usually flanked by a far inferior supporting cast, John David overcame bad front offices, sometimes mediocre coaching and poor offensive lines. And largely because

of those critical factors, his skills often went unnoticed.

Except by those involved with pro football.

In a preseason game against Green Bay in 1961, John David's left leg was broken and his ankle was dislocated on an end sweep. He missed almost all of the season, and Carolyn says, "That was the first time it really hit me that he could be crippled or badly hurt."

In 1963, John David tore up his right knee in preseason and underwent surgery that sidelined him most of that year.

And yet, Green Bay's Vince Lombardi tried to make a 4-for-1 trade to obtain him before the '64 season – offering the Cardinals halfback Tommy Moore, defensive back John Symank, offensive guard Ed Blaine, and defensive tackle Ron Kostelnik.

The Detroit Lions that same year attempted to deal a skilled quarterback, Milt Plum, and star tackle, Alex Karras (the 1957 Heisman runner-up), to the Cardinals in exchange.

Houston sports columnist Mickey Herskowitz says, "Had you taken a poll of the general managers in the NFL at the time, I'm sure several would have taken John David over Jimmy Brown – because John David could really block and catch the ball."

One apparently true rumor of the day had Paul Brown of the Cleveland Browns trying to do exactly that: offering his great fullback straight up for Crow.

When John David finally was traded, at his request,

to the 49ers, his knees battered and body beaten, the Cardinals still received Abe Woodson, a talented cornerback who had led the NFL in kick-off returns three times.

In 1962, when John David scored the 17 touchdowns, New York Giants general manager Buddy Young said, "He's the finest complete football player I've ever seen. I'd have to say he's the best, with Jim Taylor of Green Bay second. They do everything and do it well. Brown and Hornung can't block with these guys."

John Brodie, one of the top passers of his era and John David's roommate as well as teammate in San Francisco, flatly maintains, "John was the premier running back in the game his first few years. He was gaining 1,000 yards for a mediocre offense in an era when people rarely gained a 1,000 even on a good team.

"People don't realize what a great pass receiver and blocker he was. He was one of the few running backs who could do it all. In San Francisco, when they needed him to play tight end, he made the switch and continued to be one of our most valuable players. It's one thing to go play it; it's another to be really good at it."

Larry Wilson, a Hall of Fame defensive back for the Cardinals, campaigned John David for the NFL Hall of Fame 20 years ago, calling him "the most dedicated, prepared, unselfish, giving and complete football player I have ever played with and coached. The only honor missing from his outstanding list of accomplishments is to be with his peers in Canton."

John David merely shrugs. The more the years have passed, the less it's mattered.

"I know this may be hard for some people to believe," he says, "but I just don't care all that much if I'm in the pro football Hall of Fame. I think I'm in a category of old-timers now, and ... What it gets down to is the people who played with me and against me know what I could do and how much I gave to the game. That's about all the satisfaction I need."

John David entered pro football one year before Vince Lombardi was named head coach of the Green Bay Packers, two before the birth of the Dallas Cowboys expansion franchise and Lamar Hunt's American Football League.

Jim Brown, still perhaps the greatest ball carrier in

NFL history, led the league in rushing for the first time in 1958. And though he would do so seven more times over the next nine years, a new era of talented backs also ushered in Hornung and Taylor in Green Bay, Moore in Baltimore, and later, Sayers with the Bears.

John David was on that quality level, but the Cardinals were a miserable lot. Otherwise, they would not have had the rights to the first draft pick in 1958. Through a bit of fortune, they also owned the bonus choice, awarded to one team a year in an order determined by lot.

Desperately in need of a quarterback, they decided to use one of the picks to pluck Rice's King Hill. Not desperately in need of a running back – they had Ollie Matson – the Cardinals so coveted John David they used the other first pick on him (and dealt Matson to the Rams for nine players).

The Cardinals signed their hot prospect for $15,000. At 22, John David earned what Bear Bryant was making at Texas A&M before taking a $3,000 a year raise to go to Alabama.

"I remember being so shocked when they published John David's salary in the papers," Carolyn says. "Back then, it was like sex – people just didn't talk about it because it didn't seem to be anybody else's business."

Each year, the Crows lived on half of what they made and stored away the rest. In 1958, that meant $7,500 in the savings account.

"Pro ball was a breeze compared to our college days," John David says. "We didn't have any financial worries for the first time. Plus, Carolyn and I were a little older, and more carefree."

At the peak of his game, he earned $30,000 with the Cardinals and was earning $45,000 with the 49ers when he retired after the 1968 season. San Francisco tried to lure him back with a two-year, $100,000 contract, plus an assistant coaching job upon retirement.

But John David had never sat on the bench in his life, not healthy, and he wasn't about to face that possibility down the road.

The NFL consisted of only 12 pro teams with 33-man rosters in 1958.

"There weren't many players, but it was a snap," John

John David and son, Johnny, enjoying Christmas in Houston in 1960.

record of the 1950's decade in '56.

After the move to St. Louis, the Cardinals again played in a baseball park, Sportsman's Park, and again played in the shadows of a baseball team, the Cardinals during the Stan Musial era.

But John David made his mark. Robert Burns of the St. Louis Globe Democrat wrote, "Not only is Crow the best all-around back, one of the top men in the league, but he's the natural and accepted leader of the Cardinals."

Just as he had been at Springhill, Texas A&M and later in San Francisco, John David was a captain of the Cardinals. He never played on a team that he did not captain at some point.

But the adjustment from College Station to Chicago was a bit sobering for the Crows, at first.

In the second game of the 1958 season, and first home game in Chicago, John David raced 83 yards for a touchdown the first time he touched the ball – still the longest run in Cardinals history.

That day, a teenage gang extended its own unofficial South Side greeting. Carolyn had watched the game from the stands with the other players' wives and family members. After the game, the lights were turned off as the crowd filtered out.

Still in the stands, a half-dozen gang members surrounded about that many wives of players and coaches.

"I thought it was a joke at first," Carolyn says. "I'd never seen a gang before. But then they started pushing us against the rails and penning us against the wall. We started yelling for help, but only one man tried and they started beating him up.

"It was scary. One wife who came from a big city began hitting them with her purse. Finally, a little ush-

David says, "because you only played offense or defense after the season started."

The Cardinals shared second billing on the city's tough South Side with Comiskey Park's true darlings, the "Go-Go" White Sox of Luis Aparicio, Nellie Fox and Minnie Minoso, who won their first American League pennant in 40 years in 1959.

Baseball's Cubs were also a city treasure, and the Bears of Willie Gallimore and Bill George were the Sunday favorites in Chicago. The Cardinals had won the NFL championship in 1947 but posted their only winning

er came up and pulled out a switch-blade and said, 'Follow me,' and he led us to the dressing room area."

John David picks up the story from here:

"I'm going into the dressing room feeling high and mighty and on top of the world after that 83-yard run, when a policeman brings in a man whose face looks like hamburger meat. The man said he was just trying to protect some ladies after the lights had been turned out too quickly. I saw the looks of the guy and thought, "My God, I hope Carolyn wasn't in that bunch." Well, she was, and it scared her half to death.

"The next day, I went downtown to the offices of the team president, Walter Woofner. I told him what had happened and said, 'This kind of thing doesn't go on in Springhill, La., or College Station, Tex. I'm going home because I don't want to live somewhere where when a woman calls for help, nobody answers. Carolyn is going to be coming to my games, and I'm not going to have her hurt.' "

Walter Woofner rearranged the seating, placing the wives and families near the locker rooms.

Not that life was ugly in Chicago. Carolyn enjoyed taking little Johnny to the park. There was always something to do. And, they only lived there six months; the other six months John David worked for a drilling company in Houston. He later bought into a construction company in Pine Bluff, Arkansas, where Harry and Velma had also moved.

The first year in St. Louis, five former Aggies played for the Cardinals: Crow, Ken Beck, John Tracey, Bobby Joe Conrad and Kenneth Hall. The Cardinals took a hard look at a Southwest Conference backfield of Hill at quarterback, Crow and Hall at running back, and Conrad at flanker.

John David scampers for a touchdown against the Bears in 1966.

After a spell in Canada's crazy razzle-dazzle league, Ken Hall did indeed get a look in the NFL, but a knee injury wrecked him. The highlight of his career was a 104-yard kickoff return for the Houston Oilers and a 31.2 kickoff return average in 1960. Both records outlasted the Oilers' stay in Houston. Hall won an American Football League championship ring that year.

Injuries, of course, are the bane of all pro football players. John David's left shoulder was a constant problem, always slipping out of the socket. He learned to pop it back in himself. He underwent several knee surgeries; the joints are worn, and someday the knee will likely have to be replaced.

John David did not get to play in the annual College

All-Star Game following his Heisman year because he passed out during workouts and had to be put in isolation. For the next few years, he was given sugar shots and IVs before games. A thoughtful member of the Cardinals staff used to leave two Hershey bars and a Coca-Cola at his locker before each game, until John David politely explained that wasn't really quite sufficient.

Then, too, there was the eye.

"My eye was a bigger problem in pro football," John David says. "We only had the one bar and chin strap in college, but pro helmets had two bars, making it tougher on my vision. Also, a lot of the stadiums had baseball infield dirt in certain areas, so I had big problems with mud and with dusty infields. My eye was always tearing up. I'd go to the sidelines and just pour water into it."

Against Detroit one Thanksgiving Day, a defender flicked out an arm and jabbed John David's left eye – the one that wouldn't close – with a fingernail.

John David writhed in agony, blood seeping from his eyeball.

"Of all the broken bones and knee problems," he says, "I've never felt pain like that eye injury.

"It took four stitches in the eyeball to sew it up. Sleeping became a little tough because every time my eyelid came down across those stitches I blinked."

A plastic surgeon in St. Louis took a tendon out of one of John David's legs and helped pull the eye up, easing his facial paralysis and eliminating some of the dust. Several years later, a doctor in Alabama actually relaxed the eye enough to close, at last.

Probably the biggest difference in John David as a pro was his willingness to do anything to pump up his teammates – particularly when the squad was struggling.

"Coach Bryant thought rah-rah was horseshit unless the guy was a bona fide gorilla-killer," Charlie Krueger says. "You had to show you could do it before he'd let you jump around and talk about it. But in the pros, John David was real active. In San Francisco, he helped Jack Christiansen (head coach at the time) and Brodie in meetings. John David definitely had a sense of what worked."

Brodie unabashedly maintains, "John David is the most thoroughly prepared and complete professional I ever played with in 17 years with the 49ers. With his skills,

it made him awesome. He also was the most willing teammate I had – willing to sacrifice for the benefit of the team."

Brodie loves to tell the story of how John David, at tight end and obviously a couple steps slower following several surgeries, still out-smarted and out-gutted people. Playing against the 49ers' bitter rivals, the Rams, in the Los Angeles Coliseum in 1965, Crow returned to the huddle following a pass play and told Brodie:

"Call that same play. I'm gonna split the linebackers and then cut underneath Eddie Meador (the free safety). You've got to get me the ball between the 30 and 40 on their side of the field in order to score. If I get it on this side of the field, they'll run me in the ground."

Brodie heard the part about the 30- and 40-yard lines, but not on their side of the field. He threw too soon, and watched a piece of football poetry.

"John David took the ball over his shoulder and got all the way down to the one-yard line before they tackled him," Brodie says. "He still fell into the end zone for the score and was so damn tired he could hardly get up. He hadn't really looked forward to battling it for 60 or more yards, but he did it. John David always got it done."

While on the West Coast, the Crows lived in Redwood City, 40 minutes south of San Francisco. They watched the hippies on television news and the Vietnam War protests but seldom came face to face with the flower children of the 1960's. Of course, when the team bus was headed for Kezar Stadium, it cruised right down Haight Ashbury and past the hippies in the park.

"I couldn't relate to them, but they didn't bother me," John David says. "It was late in my career, and I was cool by then."

For five years at training camp and on road trips, Brodie was his roommate and became one of John David's dearest friends.

"We found that nice combination between being responsible and wild," Brodie says. "We had an awful lot of fun. He was probably the single most instrumental factor in my becoming a top player.

"We once made a deal in our wills. Whoever goes first, the other has to endow a certain amount of money to throw a party and invite all the right people. We both know who those would be."

Of course, John David's enthusiasm did not involve spiking the ball or dancing in the end zone or strutting around and crowing with his helmet on his hip. Well, he did throw the ball into the stands once – on his first trip back to St. Louis after being traded. But it wasn't spontaneous. He predicted it.

John David, who on 72 other occasions simply flipped the ball to an official after scoring, went to then-head coach Dick Nolan on the sidelines and asked to run a specific pass pattern. Then he told Nolan, "If it works and I go into the end zone, I'm throwing the ball into the stands. I know we'll be penalized; I just want you to know that right now."

Sure enough, he scored, then hurled the ball in celebration.

"My teammates just busted out laughing," John David says. "They thought I'd gone crazy. Nobody did that kind of stuff back then, but it became a fad shortly after that."

Brodie says, "It was so out of character, like Hale Irwin running around high-fiving everybody at the U.S. Open. John just wanted the Cardinals to know he really wasn't the reason the team was losing."

Pardee says John David also changed an NFL rule – the crack-back block.

In another tough game against the Rams, he was lined up at flanker and put in motion so that he could come back and side-swipe legendary defensive end Deacon Jones, who outweighed John David by 50 pounds.

The first time they ran the play, Jones was livid and warned Crow he'd better lay off.

The next time, John David nailed him even harder, then entered the huddle and said to Brodie, "If it's all the same to you, I'd just as soon you line me up over on the left side for a while. There's a guy over here on the right side who's just a little pissed, and I don't think I've got my gun on me."

But a few plays later, Brodie had John David flanked out to the right again, this time in front of Pardee. Deacon Jones yelled for Pardee to switch with him, and on the snap Jones took a mighty swing at John David's head.

But John David ducked, then drove his helmet into the big man's chin, knocking Deacon Jones to the ground.

John David ran back to the huddle and said to Brodie, "Jesus Christ. I've never seen anybody that mad. He's gonna murder me. I ain't kidding; keep me on the OTHER SIDE."

The 49ers did not switch him to tight end until his final season, in 1968. John David had already announced it would be his final one, no matter what. He was only 37 yards shy of one of the milestones of that day – 5,000 yards rushing in a career.

But the 49ers' tight end, Bob Windsor, was drafted into the Army, and Crow accepted the shift for the good of the team. Later in the season, the coaches decided to reinstall him at running back so that he could reach the milestone.

Typically, John David responded, "If I have to run the ball just so I can get into some record book, I'd rather keep the 4,963 I know I got by playing football. It'd be nice to make 5,000, but it ain't that big a deal."

Every facet of John David and Carolyn's life blossomed during that pro decade – their lifestyles, their personalities, their family. Before the 1961 season, when Johnny was 6, the first of two daughters was born – Anna Lisa. Four years later while John David was in his first training camp with the 49ers, Carolyn gave birth to Jeannie in Pine Bluff.

They were always on the move, yet very committed to the family. The home was always more important than the house.

Anna Lisa, married and a school teacher in Tyler, says, "I was a football brat the way some kids are military brats. We would go to school a half year in Pine Bluff and a half year in San Francisco, and we never thought of it as being a big deal.

"As a child, I just remember my dad having a job where sometimes he came home hurt. I knew my dad played football, but we didn't talk about it that much at home. At home, his family was everything, and still is. The Heisman was something my mom would put a scarf on at Christmas time. That's all I knew about it."

"I've lived in Tyler for 13 years," Anna Lisa says, "but I still consider home wherever my parents are living.

While visiting New York City in 1958, John David visits backstage with entertainer Steve Lawrence (middle) and his wife, Edie Gormé (second from left), and friends.

When I call them up to say we're coming to visit, I still tell them I'm coming home."

Finally, the day came when John David realized his family needed him to put away football completely.

"My knees were bad and Carolyn was having to choose between her husband's football games and Johnny's Pop Warner League in California," John David says. "Johnny's team went all the way to the championship game in L.A.

"Ultimately, we made the decision – and I do mean WE – to quit playing because of our children. Everything Carolyn and I did was based on our entire family's needs, not just on ours."

He adds, "I would have made more money today, but I'm glad I played when I did. When the owners of pro football started signing players and giving bonuses based on individual achievements in a team sport, it ceased to be a team sport.

"All the running back does when he scores is his job, just like the guard. There's no need to single out one anymore than the other.

"I'm proud of the fact that I started the last pro game I played. I didn't want to hang on. I loved the game. I'd seen too many guys become bitter late in their careers, and I wasn't going to do that."

San Francisco columnist Ron Fimrite wrote that John David had "a Gary Cooperishness" about him that final season – "the lone sheriff facing the firing squad."

Fimrite continued, "He is, in short, the sort of fierce competitor and loyal teammate one reads about in   fiction."

Which is fitting. John David has always maintained he's enjoyed a storybook existence – thanks to his family, and the game he paid back in kind.

John David congratulates all-America halfback Johnny Musso on the Alabama sidelines in 1969.

CHAPTER ELEVEN

A New Football Journey

When all was said and done, John David's road back to College Station wound through three pro cities, two off-season homes, a stint on Bear Bryant's staff at Alabama, stretches as an assistant coach with the Cleveland Browns and San Diego Chargers, five beneficial years as athletic director and head coach at Northeast Louisiana, brief careers as a Coors distributor and an insurance salesman – and then Jackie Sherrill called.

John David could not have been more thrilled to be returning to Texas A&M in 1983, the 25-year anniversary of his Heisman, than if Coach Elmer himself had extended the invite.

John David (second from left, first row) joins a gathering of the Texas All-Pro Team at Texas Stadium in the mid-1970's.

Elmer Smith, by the way, was inducted into the Arkansas Hall of Fame in 1967. John David was in attendance, as was Bear Bryant. John David told reporters, "It's been 10 years since I played for him, but right now if Coach Bryant told me to run through that wall over there, I'm sure I'd give it a try."

A few months later, Gene Stallings led the Aggies to the Southwest Conference title and a victory over Bryant in the 1968 Cotton Bowl Classic. In a show of support for their alma mater, John David, several of the Junction Boys, and others who had played for Bear at A&M cheered for Stallings' squad that New Year's Day.

"I never wanted Coach Bryant or his team to ever get beat," John David says, "but I certainly wanted A&M to win. Later, I heard that somebody asked Coach Bryant how he felt when he saw me standing on the A&M sidelines, and he said, 'That's where he should have been; that's his school.' "

Life after pro ball is often an extremely difficult transition. Divorce rates soar in the first two years of a player's retirement. Athletes can't find their niche away from the arena, and wives can't quite figure out who it was they married.

But the Crows were finally getting tired of moving around so much. In Pine Bluff, John David bought into an insurance company and still had the construction company. Johnny was in junior high, and the two girls were growing fast. Pine Bluff appeared to be the place they would finally settle.

But early in 1969, the finality of John David's playing days began to sink in. The more it sunk, the more fidgety John David became.

Once, a group of friends in Pine Bluff organized a bus run to Fayetteville to watch a University of Arkansas home game. They urged John David and Carolyn to join them, but John David had no interest in watching from the stands.

"I finally got the urge and called Coach Bryant in Alabama and asked if I could come visit," John David says. "I drove from Pine Bluff to Tuscaloosa that same day."

When they finished talking, Bryant told John David to go on back to his businesses, then return to Alabama for spring practice.

"I'll turn the running backs over to you, but if you're coming I want you to really coach them," Bryant said.

While coaching at San Diego, John David observes as Johnny Unitas instructs Chargers' quarterback Jessie Fretus.

That spring, Bryant was impressed enough to offer John David a full-time job. When John David said he wasn't sure, that he needed to talk with Carolyn and map out their family's future, Bryant nodded and said, "Well, you got a couple months. Don't worry."

Two weeks later, Bryant phoned wanting a decision. John David asked him for a couple of more days. Bear gave him a couple of more hours, then called back and said, "Tell Carolyn you're gonna coach. Put your house up for sale and get on down here."

John David was the running backs coach at Alabama for three years, 1969-71. The 1971 team, led by all-America Johnny Musso – perhaps Crow's favorite student – missed the national championship by an Orange Bowl loss to Nebraska.

"I loved coaching there," John David says, "but I felt the time came to move on. I didn't want people to think the job was just given me by Coach Bryant. I wanted to prove I could coach on my own."

The Cleveland Browns offered John David a job coaching the running backs, but Johnny was an All-State running back in Alabama about to begin his senior year

in high school. John David was hesitant to pick his family up and leave again.

Until one day Johnny went to him and said, "Dad, let's go for a ride."

As they coasted around town, Johnny said to his dad, "You do whatever you think is best for your career. I'm going to be there wherever ya'll go."

Sure enough, John David served as running backs coach for the Cleveland Browns, 1972-73, on Nick Skorich's staff. Cleveland made the playoffs the first year before slipping the second year. Johnny, meanwhile, repeated as an All-State prep running back, this time in Ohio.

John David watched every one of his 17-year-old boy's games that senior year, and he still proudly says, "He was a fine running back. A&M, Alabama, Georgia Tech, Arkansas, a lot of colleges wanted him."

R.C. Slocum, an assistant on Emory Bellard's staff, recruited Johnny for Texas A&M. John David's boy was tempted to return to his original home, but he finally told his dad, "I'm afraid I won't be able to live up to their expectations."

John David coached at Northeast Louisiana for five seasons, where he built a winning program.

When Johnny visited Alabama, he met with Coach Bryant and asked him point-blank, "Coach, have you seen me play?"

"Naw, I haven't," Bear admitted.

"Have you seen me on film?"

"Naw, Johnny, but other coaches have."

"I would like for you to, and if you don't like what you see I'll understand."

That night, Bryant pulled out films of Johnny's high school games, then phoned the Crow house and said, "Johnny, I've watched the films. Now get your butt down here where you belong."

So Johnny Crow played football for Paul Bryant, al-beit a gentler, more forgiving Bear than the one who had coached his dad. Johnny liked Alabama enough to stay there after graduation, and to start his family there.

Paul Bryant Jr., now a businessman in Alabama, was 9 years old when his daddy began coaching the Aggies. College Station was so small he could ride his bike anywhere he needed to go. He was always hanging around the practice field and locker room; and, of course, he remembers what a hit little Johnny had been in Aggieland as a small boy.

"Even when Johnny was real little, and then later as a man, he always walked like his daddy," Paul Jr. says. "It was uncanny. He wasn't as fast as his daddy, but his feet were always low to the ground. Even the way he stood was exactly like John David stood. He was a fine football player on some really good Alabama teams. He was Tony Nathan's backup as a Wishbone halfback, and he played a lot."

Meanwhile, John David accepted the all-important offensive coordinator's job under Tommy Prothro with the San Diego Chargers. Quarterback Dan Fouts was just emerging as one of the game's great passers; and, along with rookie running sensation Don Woods, Crow's offense showed flashes of brilliance. The defense, however, was weaker than talk-show hype, and the Chargers finished 5-9 in 1974.

In 1975, an early injury sidelined Fouts for the year. Woods went down after two games. When John David switched to a more conservative attack, trying to run the clock and keep the defense off the field, the fans and media grew restless. San Diego went 2-12.

John Brodie says, "John David was a great student of the game, and he could have been a great coach. But the game changed; players changed. And not for the better."

When Northeast Louisiana offered John David the athletic director/head football coach position, John David and Carolyn and the two girls picked up again and headed back very near to where John David was born.

At Northeast, John David became the first Heisman Trophy winner to be named head coach of a college program.

The youngest daughter, Jeannie, a flight attendant living in a St. Louis suburb, says, "I was 3 years old when Dad retired as a player. I used to sleep every night in a 49ers jersey, but I remember him more as Coach Crow because that's what everybody called him when I was growing up."

Jeannie is married to Ken Pietrowiak, who played football at Kentucky for Jerry Claiborne – a Bryant assistant at A&M. Anna Lisa, the older daughter, met her husband-to-be, Jay Stenklyft, at Northeast.

John David gradually turned around the dilapidated program. Northeast went 2-9 the first two years; but, by 1980, when John David stepped down, the school went 7-4 and beat Northwestern on national television.

"We felt we brought Northeast up a notch or two," John David says. "Louisiana Tech was the big rival, and we beat them two of the last three. We helped build a new stadium and get the program rolling in the right direction, but a Coors Beer Distributorship came open in the spring of 1980 for the Northeast Louisiana area, and it had a chance to be real lucrative."

It might have been, too, but John David had never actually had a full-time, year-round job. He felt out of place in corporate environs, and in April 1983, he left to become a State Farm insurance agent in Tyler.

Four months later, Jackie Sherrill, athletic director and head coach at A&M, called, wondering if John David would return as associate athletic director.

"I made a quick visit and stayed at the Memorial Student Center," John David says. "I hadn't been back in 25 years. I walked across the A&M campus one day, and it was just heart-warming. The students were so nice, smiling and saying hello, obviously not knowing who I was. They were just so friendly."

John David, at 48, returned to Aggieland as associate athletic director of everything except football.

"I saw people I hadn't seen in 25 years," he says. "And I had been out of athletics almost three years. I felt back in my element."

When Sherrill ran into trouble with the NCAA and departed, John David was elevated to athletic director in December 1988.

John David told school officials they could go outside to hire a young coach, like LSU's Mike Archer; or they could bring back a great Aggie like Jack Pardee, who had coached the Washington Redskins and Houston Oilers; or they could move up one of Sherrill's assistants.

"I felt R.C. Slocum was the guy for the job," John David says. "He was the hardest-working, most knowledgeable coach on Sherrill's staff, and he knew the Aggies. I wanted that continuity."

While Slocum's Aggies were winning on the football field, John David's four years as athletic director was also highlighted by a major upgrade of women's athletics. He was actually a Title IX pioneer, turning A&M into a model for women's programs.

As with any AD position on any campus, the job had its ups and downs. John David says, "It was very rewarding – and very trying, too."

John David, Bobby Layne (middle) and Doak Walker (right) at the Cotton Bowl's 50th Anniversary celebration.

In May 1993, he resigned, and in a partnership led by Paul Bryant Jr., bought into the first pari-mutuel dog track in Texas – Gulf Greyhound Park, in LaMarque, not far from Houston.

But he never did leave the Aggies. Wally Groff, the new athletic director, asked John David to stay aboard as director of athletic development. He began his fifth year in that capacity in the fall of 1997, at age 62.

As with anybody who's lived six decades and counting, death has reared its ugly head on more than one occasion. Grandparents, aunts and uncles, Coach Billy Baucum, Coach Elmer, all are gone. A sister's daughter died in 1980.

Bear Bryant was 69 when his heart stopped beating in 1983. The funeral was so huge that Carolyn gave up her seat so that Johnny could attend with John David.

"I'm convinced fate brought John David and Coach Bryant together at A&M," Carolyn says. "They were just so right for each other; it's fitting they spent the same four years there."

After the funeral, Paul Jr. donated $100,000 to Texas A&M for a scholarship fund for the children and grand-children of the Aggies who played – and stayed – at A&M during the Bryant regime. The interest keeps the en-dowment rolling.

"I wrote the check," Paul Jr. says, "but I knew Poppa wanted it that way for A&M — and Alabama. The chil-dren of 79 former Alabama players have gone to college off the endowment. At A&M, it's being handed down to the grandchildren now."

In 1990, Harry Crow, a firm, hard-working man who became a proud papa, died at age 78. Velma passed away in 1995 at 83.

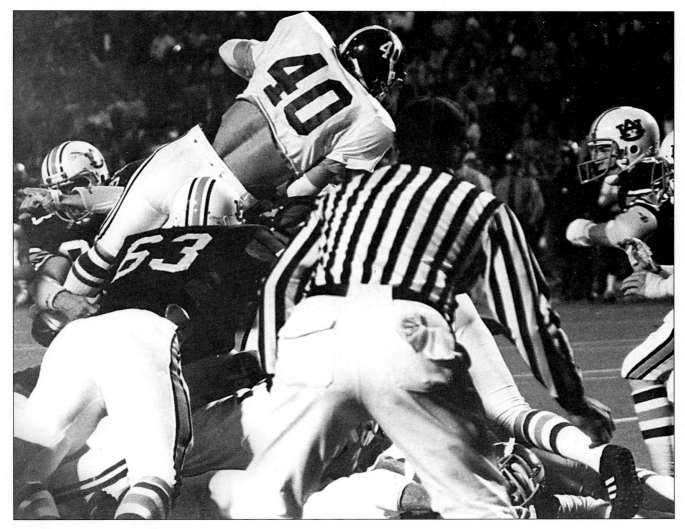

Johnny Crow, who played for Coach Bryant at Alabama in the mid-1970's, soars over the Auburn defense.

All were extremely personal, sad moments for John David and Carolyn. But nothing matches the shocking death of John David Crow Jr.

One evening in 1994, Johnny dropped off his two daughters, Christa Marie and Sara Beth, at a party not far from their home in Birmingham. On his way home, he noticed one of his hubcaps spinning off in the highway ahead.

He pulled over and got out of his car to retrieve it. Apparently, a large truck shielded him from seeing the automobile in the next lane.

Johnny was 39 years old.

"The natural progression of life teaches you that you will lose people older than you," John David says. "But when we lost Johnny, it tore a part of my heart out. It will always be the biggest tragedy of my life. With that one exception, my life would have been perfect."

When John David received the phone call, he got in touch with one of his dearest friends, Don Adams, who owns a private plane.

"I could hardly get the words out," John David says. "Don was very kind and caring. He said, 'The plane will be ready in 15 to 30 minutes, as soon as I can get in touch with the pilot.' Carolyn and I were in Alabama in no time."

Johnny Crow was buried in Birmingham. His wife,

John David and the 1976 class of inductees into the College Football Hall of Fame.

Janice, and children still live there.

Carolyn says, "He was a strong person with a big heart. He never had that stigma of being the son of a famous father. I will always cry over the loss of Johnny."

The baby boy had softened the harsh scenery of Bear Bryant's Aggieland – giggling, running around the track, reaching out for Mrs. Bryant, being handed around the training room by his daddy and other players like a sack of groceries. Johnny's parents weren't much older than his own daughters are today when the three of them did College Station together in those gritty 1950's.

Charlie Krueger says, "Little Johnny was a peach. He was a big part of it all."

"After he grew up and I stopped playing football," John David says, "we got to play some golf together and enjoy each other. He was such an upbeat person. Every

now and then, I'll still think, 'I've got to call Johnny and tell him something,' before I realize he's not here. Or I'll set up a golf match and think, 'I need to bring Johnny along,' and then it comes to me he's not here."

Bobby Joe Conrad is a judge in Bosque County these days. Jack Pardee retired to his farm near Hearne, just up Highway 6 from College Station. Players like Dennis Goehring and Loyd Taylor and Marvin Tate also stayed around the Bryan/College Station area and helped the former outpost grow into a small beehive community. Charlie Krueger is the self-proclaimed fly-fish champion of Northern California; John Brodie, one of the top players on the Celebrity Golf Tour.

Four years after winning a national championship at Alabama, Gene Stallings retired. In August 1997, he joined an effort in Dallas to dome and refurbish the Cotton Bowl Stadium. Time, as always, moves on.

Some of their friends are buying recreational vehicles these days and hitting the road. Carolyn figures they lived their lives in reverse; she and John David are perfectly happy staying at home. Or visiting their children and grandchildren.

Anna Lisa says, "I can't talk to my daddy at anytime without him telling me he loves me. His family is everything. The love he has for his grandchildren is so wonderful."

Jeannie says, "I used to ask him, 'Can I watch some game films? I never got to see you play.' He finally let me look at some old reel to reels. I just thought, 'Wow! You were so young!' "

When Carolyn and John David moved into their new home in August 1996 – perhaps the last of some 20 moves in 43 years of marriage – he had one request about where to put things.

They have a beautiful portrait of each of their three children at the age of 3.

"John David wanted them hung in the hallway," Carolyn says, "so he can tell them goodnight on his way to bed. He does it, too. Every night."

John David's office on the first floor of the Rudder Tower places him smack in the middle of Texas A&M University. He lunches on occasion at the Memorial Student Center and is a familiar face around campus, when he's not playing golf and raising money for the school.

"He's the dangest competitor on the golf course you'll ever want to see," R.C. Slocum says. "He can make par from anywhere. He never lets up on a hole, regardless of his lie."

Asked if his players today realize the silver-haired man in their midst is the great John David Crow, Slocum says, "They see the Heisman in the trophy case and that registers with some of them, and I mention his name from time to time. But in reality, they don't have any idea."

John David probably prefers it that way. His playing days give him fond memories and warm friendships, but he's never been one to wallow in the past.

He's not very good with street names when explaining how to get to his still-new home, but he knows the birth dates and exact ages of his three children and five grandchildren — Christa Marie, Sara Beth, Anthony,

David and Tommy — because those are the numbers he holds dear.

One sister, Yvonne, lives near Beaumont. She says every now and then someone is surprised to learn she's related to John David.

"I tell them I never did wear a sign around my neck announcing the fact," Yvonne says.

The older sister, Doris Ann, lives in Colorado. One of her children once asked his uncle for an autograph.

"You don't need my autograph," John David said kindly. "You've got me."

Raymond Crow coached some football at Lamar Tech. He lives in South Texas and says, "I am very proud of my brother."

In May 1997, the Mark Dennard/John David Crow Celebrity Golf Tournament was staged in College Station. The event was so huge it included 350 participants.

Players included Hall of Famers Dick Butkus and Gayle Sayers, and college greats Tommy Nobis and Glenn Davis, and a slew of Aggies from all generations.

A 12-handicapper, John David played a little golf and – in part because his good name was attached to the event – helped raise $190,000 for several Brazos Valley charities.

The good Lord willing, John David will wake up one morning in May 1998, and drive a golf cart a mere half-mile from his garage to the first tee at Pebble Creek Country Club for the next Mark Dennard/John David Crow tournament.

Afterward, if habits hold up, he's likely to drive the cart back home and, hungry for a bite to eat, walk past the only obvious reminder of his football yesterdays – a trophy of a running back stiff-arming an imaginary tackler.

Carolyn will join him in the kitchen, as usual, and they'll rummage through the refrigerator for sandwich fixings.

John David Crow, who overcame a freakish accident caused by his own umbilical cord and went on to become the greatest Aggie of them all, will be home again with the former Carolyn Gilliam, Miss Lumberjack of 1954, the prettiest gal in Louisiana – and, as John David says, "still the prettiest gal in Bryan/College Station."

Ten to Remember

JOHN DAVID CROW

to

Texas College Football Legend **JOHN DAVID CROW**

Jack Pardee (32) hurdles the LSU line for a touchdown in the second quarter. Pardee would finish the game with two TD's.

A&M's Young Sophs Romp Over LSU, 28-0

By George Kellam
Fort Worth Star-Telegram

Dallas, Sept. 24, 1955

Inspired, no doubt, by the stock car races which roared unmuffled round a race track just outside the Cotton Bowl Saturday night, Texas A&M roared past LSU, 28-0, before 17,000 spectators.

John David Crow and Jack Pardee were the hot rods who led the Aggies to their first victory since A&M beat Georgia, 6-0, in the third game of the A&M's 1954 season. This marks the end of an eight-game losing skein, and might well be the beginning of many happy weekends for the old grads of Aggieland.

Crow ran 77 and eight yards for third and fourth-quarter touchdowns respectively, after Pardee had plunged four and two yards for first and second-quarter counters, respectively. The Aggies gave the Tigers a fierce beating in every department, their vicious line play creating LSU fumbles and their pass defense picking off desperation aerials.

Crow averaged 10 yards a carry, lugging 13 times for 130 yards. Pardee carried eight times, for 91 yards and quarterback Donnie Grant carried nine times for 49 yards to pace A&M ball carriers.

Texas A&M fumbled the ball away on its first play of the game on its own 48, LSU's Durwood Graham recovering Jim Wright's bobble. But Gene Stallings, who played a tremendous game from his left end post for the Aggies, regained possession for A&M three plays later when he intercepted Matt Burns' second pass of the game and returned it seven yards to the Aggie 49.

A&M went 51 yards in 10 plays for the first-quarter touchdown, fullback Jack Pardee punching into the end zone from four yards out with 7:33 gone in the period. Right half Loyd Taylor added the extra-point kick to make it 7-0. Left half, John Crow got the march started with a 13-yard romp over right tackle on the second play from scrimmage. Taylor scatted for 12 more on the next play. After Crow lost two yards and Wright overshot Stallings with a pass, Taylor took a pitchout around left end behind Jack Powell's blocking for 11 yards to the 14. Crow made one, then Taylor caught Wright's wobbly pass on the five for a gain of eight more. Crow made one then Pardee scored.

The Aggies swarmed 99 yards in eight plays of the second-quarter score at 7:35 of the period, Pardee diving over from the two and Taylor again booting the extra point.

The drive started from the one-yard line. Tiger Bill Smith's punt from the LSU 19 bounced over Crow's head on the LSU 20. Crow picked it up on about the 10 and pulled a criss-cross handoff to Taylor going west. Ted Paris dropped Taylor, who had faded back for running room, on the one-yard line.

Taylor slashed out to the five, Crow made four yards and Pardee chipped in with seven and then four to the

The Aggies scored four touchdowns on the ground against LSU. John David carried for 130 yards on 13 carries and 2 TD's.

20. Taylor darted for five and then Pardee broke over right tackle for 65 yards to the LSU 10 where Enos Parker and O.K. Ferguson pulled him down. Stallings led the way, Crown slashed over left guard for eight yards and then Pardee dived over for the touchdown, making it 14-0.

The Tigers tore and slashed at the Aggie line but never mustered a serious first-half threat.

A&M drove from its 24 to the LSU 45 with the third-quarter kickoff only to stall. After Taylor returned Bill Smith's punt 11 yards to the Aggie 23, Crow broke over left guard, cut right about 10 yards deep in the Tiger secondary, then set sail southward, down the west sideline with Taylor affording protection. Taylor kicked the extra point and at 6:29 of the period it was 21-0, A&M.

A comedy of errors then followed. A&M intercepting two LSU passes and Stallings recovered a Mays' fumble on the Tiger eight-yard line, but the Aggies were unable to turn any of the three enemy miscues into touchdowns.

to the A&M 20-yard line for the Tigers' second best of-fensive showing of the night. Gene Henderson's inter-ception of M.C. Reynolds' pass on the Aggies' 30 stopped the march.

Grant fumbled the ball away for A&M on the 50, with Tiger Alvin Aucion recovering on the LSU 49. From here the Tigers drove to the Aggie two-yard line where time ran out.

The outcome gives Texas A&M a 1-1 record for the season, the Aggies having lost to UCLA in their opener, 21-0.

SCORE BY QUARTERS

LSU	0	0	0	0—0
Texas A&M	7	7	7	7—28

It rained briefly at start of the fourth quar-ter and on LSU's sixth play in this period Vince Gonzales fumbled and Jack Powell re-covered for the Aggies on the Tiger 33.

The Aggies scored in 10 plays, with Crow twisting away from John Wood and Paul Reb-samen on a pitchout at right end from the two-yard line. Dudley kicked the point-after.

LSU took the kickoff and drove from its 20

Aggies Thump Texas Tech

By Gene Gregston
Fort Worth Star-Telegram

Dallas, Oct. 6, 1956

Texas A&M, with the effortless ease of a State Fair midway spieler, soundly subdued Texas Tech, 40-7, Saturday night in a Cotton Bowl Stadium football contest viewed by 26,000 fans.

Getting even for a 41-9 loss suffered in the last previous meeting of these two teams, the Cadets, employing 35 players in a variety of units, scored in every period and were never scored on in any period.

Two dishes in the six-touchdown course were served by alert, defensive recovery of Tech fumbles, leaving short-yardage sorties to the end zone, but the remaining quartet on the menu resulted from drives of 50, 83, 46 and 66 yards.

Although the Cadets frequently mixed their personnel on the field and Coach Paul (Bear) Bryant sometimes had fourth-teamers aligned with starters, it remained for the older, established hands to take care of the main business.

Halfback John Crow scored one on a 13-yard run and again on a 20-yard pass thrown by quarterback Jimmy Wright, who opened the game. Quarterback Bobby Joe Conrad scored twice on short plunges. Wright threw a 10-yard touchdown strike to halfback Don Watson, and fullback Jack Pardee thundered six yards for the final score.

Loyd Taylor, one of three Aggie regulars who did not participate because of injuries, kicked three extra points and Ed Dudley converted once.

While this exhibition, which might have earned a blue ribbon in the Farmer's booth across the way, was in progress, the hapless Red Raiders were permitted no closer than 41 yards to registering a point.

Finally, however, Tech escaped a shutout when No. 2 quarterback Duddy Hill heaved a prodigious pass to end Ken Vakey for 35 yards and a touchdown. This came with four minutes 46 seconds remaining in the game. It was consolation, however small the amount.

This simply was no contest, similar in nearly every way to the 32-0 TCU victory over Tech last fall.

The Aggies rolled to a 21-4 margin in first downs, and rushed to a ground superiority of 354-62. Tech led in the passing department, where the Raiders netted 89 yards on five completions in 12 attempts, to the Cadets' 55 yards on four connections in seven tosses.

But the Aggies still have the handy habit of hitting the overhead button at opportune times.

Individually, Pardee, again a defensive standout, was the leading ground gainer with 90 yards on 14 carries, but he shared honors with quarterback Roddy Osborne (eight for 52), Crow (six for 47) and Kenneth Hall (seven for 50), the latter showing a revival of his sweet Sugarland High running.

Up front, even with Dennis Goehring and Murray Trimble, two fine guards, sidelined with chest and rib injuries, the Cadets were in command throughout, with the ends, especially, shining bright. This is more than the Cotton Bowl lights do.

Richard Gay, the highly-touted sophomore from Louisiana who became eligible with this game, carried four times for 22 yards, and acquitted himself according to advance notice on defense.

So the Aggies now are three-fourths of the way through the preliminary schedule before entering the Southwest Conference race. They are unbeaten, and actually unpressed, in a trio of games and have a date with Houston next weekend before plunging into title play against the Frogs.

SWC member-elect Texas Tech, who is at its lowest ebb since DeWitt Weaver assumed the coaching reins, has lost three straight and next meets West Texas State.

SCORE BY QUARTERS

Texas Tech	0	0	0	7—7
Texas A&M	14	7	13	6—40

Dennis Goehring, an all-America guard in 1956.

Taylor's Kick Tumbles Frogs, Aggies Stymie TCU, 7-6, in Near Hurricane

By Flem Hall
Fort Worth Star-Telegram

College Station, Oct. 10, 1956

By the margin of Loyd Taylor's extra-point kick for point after a fourth quarter touchdown, the Texas A&M Aggies toppled TCU, 7-6, here this storm-tossed Saturday afternoon in a blood and thunder football game started before a capacity crowd of 42,000 and finished with about half that many drenched spectators in the Kyle Field stands.

Winds up to an estimated 90 miles an hour and a downpour of rain handicapped both teams throughout the first half which was scoreless.

The Aggies threw one pass during the wet, slippery afternoon, but it was good for their one touchdown.

The TCU Frogs, who had figuratively hung on the lip of the scoring cup throughout the near hurricane, scored in the third quarter when O'Day Williams made a spectacular one-handed catch in the end zone of a Chuck Curtis pass.

Harold Pollard's place kick for the extra pont popped up a bit wide of the south goal posts.

(Top to bottom) Jimmy Wright, Loyd Taylor, John David and Jack Pardee led A&M to a record of 9-0-1 in 1956.

Don Watson, the 150-pound senior halfback from Franklin, who killed the Frogs last year, 19-16, with a fourth-quarter 51-yard touchdown run, sparked the attack.

First, he got the ball for the Aggies by making a magnificent leaping interception in his own end zone of a pass that was almost in the hands of Jimmy Shofner. The catch was made so close to the sideline that the Frogs thought the intercep-tion should not have counted, but it did.

From their own 20 the Aggies struck first with John Crow around his right end for 21 yards.

Then quarterback Roddy Osborne kept for two yards.

Next, he sent Watson spinning through the middle and the little man ran, stumbled and fought his way 37 yards to the TCU 20. Crow powered for two and then swept right end again for 11. Osborne carried twice for a net loss of one yard.

Then on third down from the eight, Watson took the handoff, ran to his left and flipped a pass to Crow who was running free in the end zone.

Taylor, a junior reserve halfback from Roswell, NM, hurried into the game and with Watson holding, booted the ball for the vital extra point.

The 80-yard march was made on just five plays.

The touchdown came with nine minutes left to play.

The Frogs tried manfully, but their luck was all bad and at the end A&M had the ball on the TCU 30.

It was frustrating day all around for the Frogs. They had one touchdown called back by an offside penalty. They were denied another touchdown when an official ruled Jim Swink was stopped an inch from the goal. They missed two field goal attempts and they were rolling on the Aggie 18 when Watson made his end zone interception.

TCU threatened six times and didn't score, and had one touchdown canceled. Other drives were stopped at the one-inch line and the 2-, 16-, 24- and 20-yard lines.

But the Frogs controlled the ball, running 82 plays to A&M's 50. They had 55 rushing plays, 22 passes, three punts and two field goals to A&M's rushes, one pass and six punts.

Both teams played with a minimum of manpower. A&M used 22 players, TCU 25.

The defeat was the first for the Frogs since they were clipped, 14-13, in the Cotton Bowl by Mississippi on New Year's Day.

Trying hard to beat the gathering

storm (which was preceded by tornado warnings) the Christians took the opening kickoff and struck hard and effectively at the Aggie defenses in spite of two mistakes that cost them 20 yards in penalties. The Frogs moved 63 yards before being stopped just short of a first down on the A&M 28.

The second time they got the ball the storm had hit, but in spite of the handicap of wild win and rain. Curtis kept this passing game going well enough to move all the way from his 25 to the Aggie 3. From there Swink lanced into the end zone, but the Frogs were ruled offside. Four plays later, from the two Ken Wineburg fumbled and John Tracey recovered.

No better time or place will be found in this account to say a few words about Tracey. He was terrific — the finest of all the fine defensive hands that A&M used.

The big 6-3 and 210-pound 23-year-old sophomore from Philadelphia wasn't blocked all afternoon, and wrought havoc with all attempts by the Frogs to sweep the left side. Offensively he was highly effective. It was his blocking as much as any other one thing that enabled Crow to break for his 21 and 11-yard dashes in the winning drive.

A rash of fumbles broke out in the second quarter when the ball became caked with mud that was churned out of the emerald turf.

On the first exchange of the muffs, Norman Hamilton (who proved himself the best lineman of the field with a long string of extraordinary plays) recovered an Osborne fumble on the Aggie 8. Curtis fumbled but recovered for no gain. Swink slashed for five yards and then appeared to go across the goal line, but the ball was placed down an inch or two away from the goal line.

The Aggies were offside, but there was no room for a penalty. On fourth down Swink took a handoff from Curtis and shot at the Aggie left tackle. He again appeared to penetrate before being hit and knocked back by linebacker Jack Pardee, but the official nearest the ball didn't see it that way and the ball went to the Aggies.

The storm, now at its howling best, held sway the remainder of the half.

The wind had subsided and the rain almost stopped by the time the second half opened, but conditions

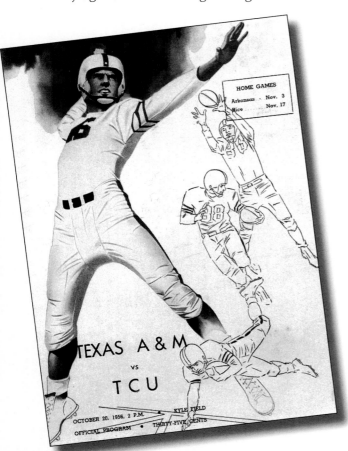

HOME GAMES
Arkansas · Nov. 3
Rice · Nov. 17

TEXAS A & M
vs
TCU

OCTOBER 20, 1956, 2 P.M. · KYLE FIELD
OFFICIAL PROGRAM · THIRTY-FIVE CENTS

Don Watson intercepts a TCU pass in the third quarter to stop a Frogs' touchdown drive.

made it impossible for the Frogs to either pass or sweep.

They broke out a new formation — a spread-T — and it worked for 40 yards on dashes by Buddy Dike and Swink before being stopped on the Aggie 17. From there Vernon Hallbeck tried his first field goal. It was such a dubbed shot that he ball rolled dead on the Aggie 5.

A few minutes later, the Frogs used a short A&M punt and a series of short gains to get back to the A&M 23 and again Hallbeck tried and failed.

It was on the subsequent Aggie series that John Nikkel recovered an Osborne fumble on the Aggie 30 and set the Frogs up for their touchdown drive.

Dike got four yards and Swink added 11. Shofner, who had replaced Wineburg when the right half was disabled on the second play of the half, sliced for two yards. A pass failed. Virgil Miller replaced Shofner and got one.

With fourth and seven fro the 12, Curtis passed over the middle to Williams. It looked as if the ball was caught after Williams went across the end line, but again the official saw it different, this time a completed pass for a touchdown.

For three minutes it looked as if the Frogs were "in" as the winner, but then another storm hit them — a red-shirted Aggie storm, and Taylor's perfect kick.

SCORE BY QUARTERS

TCU	0	0	6	0—6
Texas A&M	0	0	0	7—7

50,000 See A&M Seize 5th Victory

By Lorin McMullen
Fort Worth Star-Telegram

Waco, Oct. 27, 1956

It was a bitterly-contested battled, marked by near flare-ups and invoking of six personal fouls by busy officials who stepped off 70 yards against A&M and 55 against the Bears.

Two Baylor men were put out of the game.

Crow and Osborne led the way for the alert and quick-hitting Cadets much as they took charge in the final pay-off drive.

Crow scored one touchdown, passed to John Tracey for another and launched the winning march with a 23-yard run.

Osborne intercepted a Baylor pass to set up the first Aggie touchdown, ripped off a 17-yard run to start the second scoring drive, hurled a 32-yard pass to Don Watson to carry it to the four, and made the biggest play in the winning assault. This was a 22-yard run on which more than a half dozen Bears grabbed at him as he zigzagged to the four-yard line from where Crow went over in two tricks.

The Aggies led, 6-0, early in the second quarter, pushed ahead by 12-6 midway in the third and took the lead again after 5:40 in the fourth period, 19-13.

Their scoring drives covered 21 yards (after an interception), 95 and 63 yards.

Baylor, which once bogged down on the Aggie 5 and again on the 33, made its scores on 67 and the 36-yard advances. Larry Hickman plunged for two yards and the touchdown which tied the score at 6-6 late in the second quarter and Bobby Peters ran for 4 yards and the touchdown which enabled Baylor to go ahead, 13-12, in the first two minutes of the final period.

Arthur (Junior) Beall, with Robby Jones holding, kicked the extra point that put the Bruins out front.

Baylor, which lost ball three times on fumbles and twice on interceptions, covered two Aggie fumbles and intercepted one pass to hold the Farmers scoreless in the first quarter.

Early in the second period Osborne intercepted Jones' pass and the Aggies went 21 yards to a touchdown on six plays, with Crow's passing to Tracey in the end zone for the touchdown.

Baylor used 11 plays on its 67-yard spree for the tying touchdown, scored by Hickman, who made the last 23 yards in four carries.

When the Bears were stopped at the Aggie 5 at start of the second half, Osborne broke loose for 17 yards, ground plays carried up to Baylor's 36. Osborne then uncorked the big play.

He sent the fleet Watson down the left sideline, where he got behind Beall, caught the ball about the 15 and raced on to the four, where Jones went over to help Beall knock him out of bounds.

Then Jack Pardee, reported too wounded to be of

Bryant & Co. Celebrate Win Over Baylor

By Lorin McMullen
Fort Worth Star-Telegram

Coach Paul Bryant inhaled the brisk October air like a man who had held his breath for 60 minutes, and in an exaggerated surrender to the inevitable led reporters behind the scenes of Texas A&M's stirring, 19-13 triumph over Baylor.

"Boys," Bear pleaded with a wounded smile, "aren't you going to let us enjoy this one a minute?"

But outside the jubilant Aggie dressing room, which echoed to a lusty chorus of the "Aggie War Hymn," the circle around Bryant tightened and questions were fired with the rapidity of the charges of Saturday's opposing lines.

Bryant was asked if he made any adjustment in strategy during the intermission, which found the game tied, 6-6.

"Well," he drawled, "you have to tell them something or they don't think you've been watching the game."

Then he shrugged and added, despairingly. "We used a few flankers in the second half, that's all."

It developed that fullback Jack Pardee, bothered by a bruised shoulder, played at his own insistence.

"I have to take my hat off to Pardee," marveled the hatless, tieless and obviously exuberant Bryant.

"I thought he was going to whip me if I didn't send him in. I hadn't planned to play him at all — win, lose or draw. But I didn't want to get whipped.

"When I called the startling lineups out with Dick Gay at fullback, Pardee gave me that mean Farmer look. He bothered me constantly, so finally I sent him in so I could watch the game."

Pardee played nearly half the 60 minutes and, though below top efficiency, was a key figure in the Cadet defense.

So heady was this victory over an undefeated Baylor team that the usually evasive Bryant found it difficult to restrain himself.

"I thought John Crow was magnificent," Bryant slipped, then caught himself. "That's a pretty big adjective for me I better make that *good*."

There was no uncertainty in Bryant's mind over the grandes moment in a game that saw the tide of battle take hairpin turns.

"I was proudest when they came back to score that third touchdown and win," said Bryant, who declared he was prouder of the Aggies this week than in their upset of TCU, when he had "never been so proud of a team before."

Over the din of the "Aggie War Hymn," Bear laughingly confided "I can't carry a tune but I help them make noise."

Inside the A&M lockers where the Aggie donned their civilian uniforms of charcoal coats and gray flannel slacks, the scene was as confused as would be expected of a team that established itself the Southwest Conference title favorite.

Charlie Krueger, the Caldwell junior who played a tremendous tackle, accepted some pills from Trainer Smokey Harper and explained to a visitor, "I gotta nervous stomach."

Asked when the disorder struck him, Krueger replied, "When Baylor kicked its extra point."

Crow, the brilliant halfback who threw to John Tracey for the first touchdown and scored the winning one, offered his philosophy.

"As long as we got a chance to get the ball in the fourth quarter," Crow said, "I think we've got a chance of winning."

much help for the second straight week, made a second straight bid for stardom by bulling over the middle for the touchdown. Taylor missed the extra-point kick to put A&M ahead, 12-6.

An 18-yard punt by Osborne gave the Bears their opportunity for a matching second touchdown and they cashed in quickly at start of the fourth.

Jones went around right end for seven yards and on the play the Aggies were fined 15 for defensive holding, giving Baylor a first down on the nine. There Reuben Saage made three against the tightly packed middle, Peters went wide to the left for two yards and on the next play slashed at left tackle for four and the tying touchdown. Beall kicked the extra point that put Baylor ahead for the first time, 13-12.

An offside on the ensuing kickoff helped the Aggies. Bill Anderson's first one went to Crow on the three, but the Bears were set back five and this time Bobby Marks received at the 18 and returned to the 37.

Crow immediately ran wide to the right, cut back and made 23 yards. Osborne kept for five yards, Crow hit right tackle for three and here the Green and Gold luck failed.

Pardee made six yards, fumbled and Baylor recovered but the official ruled the ball dead before the fumble and the Aggies kept possession on the Baylor 26.

Osborne felt like celebrating and did so with a miraculous escape act as he started toward the left, skipped and wiggled through four or five Bears as he turned up field, served back over tothe right, eluded the clutching paws of another pocket of Bears and went on for a 22-yard total to the 4.

Osborne failed on the next try, then gave to Crow for consecutive dives at left tackle and he made two yards each time for the touchdown.

Taylor kicked the point-after this time to make the score 19-13.

SCORE BY QUARTERS

Texas A&M	0	6	6	7—19
Baylor	0	6	0	7-13

Aggies Shatter Jinx, Bump Texas, 34-21

By Lorin McMullen
Forth Worth Star-Telegram

Austin, Nov. 29, 1956

Mighty Texas A&M shattered 32 years of Memorial Stadium tradition, sealed the first Aggie Southwest Conference championship since 1941 and scored the highest point total in history of the ancient series by out-gaining game the University of Texas, 34-21.

The sizzling offensive duel established A&M superiority quickly with leads which at various points grew to 13-0, 20-7 and 34-14.

But it was a much closer battle than could rightfully be expected from the down-trodden Longhorns, who entered the game with a 1-8 record and 16-point underdogs on the handicap sheets.

Texas came back with a touchdown in the closing seconds of the final quarter to pull within 13 points and was driving toward another score when Lloyd Hale intercepted Joe Clements' pass.

The Texas threats, however, served only to make it an honorable contest. The Aggies had the power and the speed to move and, with one or two possible exceptions, advanced impressively.

Despite the free scoring, there was hardly a critical juncture in the game unless the second half kickoff was singled out as a turning point. Matters already had been rather definitely established but this, at least, settled any dreams of a miraculous comeback by the fired-up Longhorns.

Bob Bryant had made a tremendous catch and short run at end of the first half and Walter Fondren had made the second of his three conversions to cut the Aggie margin to 20-14.

The poised, confident and machine-like Aggies knew this could be trouble.

So, at start of the second half when Chris Shaw boomed a kick-off into the end zone, John Crow relaxed to let the ball go by. But not Jack Pardee, the gangling, pile-driving fullback.

He stretched for the ball on the goal line, bore straight ahead through an on-rushing Orange pack inside the 20, swerved off to the left side line as he cleared the deeper defenders and headed long-gone, toward the goal line.

Only Clements kept in pursuit. They raced for some 40 yards with Pardee still a step ahead but finally Clements made his lunge and brought down the big Aggie on the 15 — an 85-yard return.

From there the Aggies scored in three plays — 4 yards by quarterback Roddy Osborne at the middle, 3 yards by Loyd Taylor at right tackle and then Pardee broke through right tackle, ran over the linebackers and scored from 8 yards out.

Taylor kicked one of his three conversions and this made it 27-14, putting A&M comfortably ahead and probably planting the first convincing thoughts in the minds of the Longhorns about the shattering of the jinx.

A few plays later Clements and Pardee were hurt on the same play and the Texas offense was sharply handicapped. Clements stayed out until late in the period but came back to make it interesting in the fourth quarter and to finish the game as the total offense leader with 139 yards on 22 plays which included nine pass completions in 15 attempts.

Pardee, ironically, finished with a modest 25 yards on eight carries, yet his 85-yard return unquestionably was the big play of the game.

Osborne carried nearly twice as often as any other player on the field and made 55 yards on 21 carries. Taylor was the top rushing gainer with 91 yards on 11 carries.

Defensively, the Aggies were paced by right guard Dennis Goehring and right end John Tracey. For Texas right guard Don Wilson, pitted against superior opposition on all sides, battled conspicuously and gummed the Aggie handoffs as they have not been harassed all season.

Bryant, Texas' brilliant sophomore end from Plainview, was as much of a standout on offense as the great Tracey was on defense. He caught two touchdown passes and barely missed on a couple of others only because of spectacular saves by Taylor, Crow or Lloyd Hale.

Pardee's long gallop came after Carl Wylie had set up one Texas touchdown with a 57-yard kick-off return and Carl Branch had made a 42-yard run for Texas.

Long Aggie plays included a 29-yard sprint by Taylor and a 33-yard Osborne-to-Marks pass maneuver.

The Aggie touchdowns came on drives of 72, 80, 50, 15 and 71 yards. Texas drives covered 80, 28, and 52 yards.

The touchdowns were scored by A&M's Crow (27 yards) Osborne (3 and 4 yards), Pardee (8 yards) and George Gillar (1 yard).

Texas connected on Walter Fondren's 43-yard run and

Clements' passes to Bryant for 14 and 10 yards.

The Aggies used eight plays for the opener, scored on their first possession as impetus was picked up on the 33-yard Osborne-Marks pass play down the left sideline. On second down from the 27, Osborne faked the belly play to Pardee, handed to the trailing Crow and he shot off right tackle for the touchdown. That was in the first six minutes of play.

The score stood 7-0 until early in the second quarter, when the Aggies used 15 plays to get their 80 yards. The three longest plays were Taylor's 29-yarder, Osborne's pass (after being tightly pocketed) to Taylor for 12 and another to Marks, who made an excellent catch for 11. This put the ball on the 26 and from there it was Osborne and Taylor on short runs to the 6, where Crow made 3 yards on an end sweep and Osborne kept through left tackle for the touchdown.

Here Taylor missed the conversion and the Longhorns changed the 13-0 score to 13-7 by going 80 yards with the next kick-off. Clements started it with a 24-yard keeper around the right side and went the same direction for 9 more.

After a pitchout to Fondren made 4 yards to the A&M 43, Fondren broke through the middle on the draw play, swerved to the left and with the aid of a timely block by Wayne Wash, dashed the 46 yards to a touchdown.

An exchange of kicks gave A&M the ball on the 50 late in the second quarter and the Cadets swarmed to a touchdown in four plays — 22 yards around end by Taylor, 21 through the middle by Crow, 3 by Osborne on a keeper and the last four by Osborne on another keeper. It was 20-7 with 90 seconds to go in the half.

Wylie took the kickoff on the 15, went up the middle and was getting away from everybody except Marks, who caught him from the rear and pulled him down after 57

John David studies a Texas defender as he sweeps right end for eight yards in the Aggies' first win in Memorial Stadium.

yards. There, Clements passed to Mike Trant for 14 and on the third straight pass play with 15 seconds remaining, hit Bryant who made an astonishing catch on the 4 and dived over at the right-field corner for the touchdown.

Two seconds were left when Fondren kicked the extra point to make it 20-14, and a ball game.

Pardee's heroics on the second-half kickoff put the game back in the bag as he capped it with his 8-yard touchdown run and the game drew out of hand midway in the third period when the Aggies went 71 yards in 13 plays for the touchdown that gave the Aggies a 33-14 lead.

In this march Gillar has a 14-yard run, Osborne passed to Crow for 22 and Gillar went 29 yards to the 4. There, on fourth down, Gillar bucked over from the 1.

Clements, who had sat out most of the third period, returned near the finish and midway in the fourth quarter got the Longhorns rolling for 52 yards in eight plays and the third touchdown.

Branch made 7 yards, Clements passed to Walsh for 10 and got a break on a heave to Fondren who took the ball after it was deflected by Marks and turned the pass play into a 22-yard gainer to the 11.

On the second play, from the 10, Clements rolled out to the left and after some delay, threw to Bryant in the end zone where he had to fight to keep from letting Pardee wrestle the ball away from him. This was seven minutes deep in the final period.

Again Texas stormed to the 19, where Hale intercepted Clements' pass to end the threat.

The 21 points was Texas' high for the season. The 13-point margin was, in a way, an upset. But the tradition sure is a goner.

SCORE BY QUARTERS

Texas A&M	7	13	14	0—	34
Texas	0	14	0	7 —	21

Aggies Stave Off Porkers, 7-6

By Gene Gregston
Fort Worth Star-Telegram

Fayetteville, Ark., Nov. 2, 1957

They were once behind and oft-beleaguered, but they are still unbeaten.

The nation's No. 1 collegiate football team foiled an ambitious Arkansas challenger, 7-6, here this cool, cloudy and dry Saturday.

And just how and why will be difficult to describe.

For 31,000 fans who must have been exhausted by the thrilling spectacle, it may even remain a mystery— and they saw it in person.

But they'll long remember the huge figure of one John David Crow, Texas A&M's magnificent halfback who capped his greatest afternoon of the current campaign by intercepting an Arkansas pass while near the Cadets' goal line.

Only a minute remained in the scintillating struggle when Crow's theft of George Walker's hard aerial shot signaled demise of the last valiant Razorback bid for victory.

Crow's role of mortician was made necessary by the day's most spectacular play, a 57-yard return of an intercepted Roddy Osborne pass by Arkansas halfback Don Horton.

He stabbed the ball on his own 16 as the Aggies were attempting to gain a first down and run out the clock. With Gerald Nesbitt as convoy, Horton sailed down the east sideline into the mild north wind.

Osborne hauled him down at the 27. A minute 35 seconds were left. Walker then passed to Horton for a first down at the 16, and Horton ran for three. Walker's second-down shoot-the-works throw to the end zone was then cut off by Crow.

Earlier in the fourth quarter, Arkansas, using the fast break, had rumbled 66 yards to the A&M 5, where third-string quarterback Freddy Akers' fourth-down field goal attempt from placement at the 12 barely flew wide to the left.

And in the third quarter the persistent Porkers chiseled out a 41-yard chunk of the harvest-brown turf down to the A&M 29, to be halted by a fumble.

But where they dominated the second half and failed to score the resourceful Razorbacks took the short end of the statistical sticking the first half, but scored.

This they managed on their third possession, and with their alternate unit quarterbacked by Don Christian on the field. Christian made the last step of a 47-yard surge with 11 minutes elapsed in the game.

But Nesbitt's kick for point was wide to the left — the Porkers weren't place-kicking "right" this day.

Still, this was the first time in seven 1957 encounters that the Aggies had been behind, and the partisan throng relished the moment and disregarded the conversion failure.

After intercepting an Arkansas pass, John David outruns a Razorback tackler for A&M's winning touchdown.

It proved to be, ultimately and after much ado about nothing, the difference.

For in the second quarter after misfiring on their second good penetration, the virile Aggies ripped 74 yards to the tying touchdown. Crow scored it, unwinding 12 big yards around right end. And Loyd Taylor kicked the winning point.

Crow, never stopped without gaining, punched out 116 yards in 21 carries as the Aggies outrushed Arkansas, 251-238. A&M also gained a 38-15 aerial advantage.

And those figures just about reflect the true differential of the teams.

And like they say, an inch is as good as a mile, because the Aggies, aided by SMU's upset of Texas, now are alone at the head of the Southwest Conference class with a 3-0 reading.

SCORE BY QUARTERS

Texas A&M	0	7	0	0—7
Arkansas	6	0	0	0—6

John David and the Aggie defense stack up Arkansas halfback Don Horton.

Crow Sparkles as Aggies Beat SMU, 19-6

By Bill Van Fleet
Fort Worth Star-Telegram

College Station, Nov. 9, 1957

John Crow sparkled with his all-American brilliance Saturday night as he led his Texas Aggie teammates to a 19-6 victory over Southern Methodist.

It was a slashing, tearing Southwest Conference football game that kept the 28,000 fans at Kyle Field in an uproar most of the way. The outcome remained in doubt until late in the fourth period when the Aggies staged a 76-yard drive in the final seven minutes.

Just a few minutes before, Southern Methodist was on the Aggie one-yard line, threatening to tie or go ahead. A fourth-down play gained only part of that final yard and the Aggies were saved.

Up to that point it was anybody's ball game, with Southern Methodist's young Don Meredith running a surprise spread formation that kept the Aggie defense loose and nervous.

The Aggies counted first, two-thirds deep in the first period, but for the first time this year failed to add the extra point.

The Ponies drove 71 yards with the ensuing kickoff, running from their regular split-T formation, and tied the score at 6-6 less than a minute deep in the second. Charlie Krueger, the star Aggie tackle, blocked the extra-point try.

It remained 6-6 at the intermission and until there was less than two minutes left in the third period before Crow capped a 65-yard drive by scoring from the two for the Aggies.

The next seven minutes were agony for the yelling Cadets and pure excitement for the rest of the people in the stands.

Jimmy Welch, the Mustang halfback from Abilene, returned the kickoff to the Pony 22, and from there Ken Lowe and Don Meredith used the spread to take the ball all the way to the A&M 1 before a fourth-down smash from the split-T failed.

That broke the Ponies' back. Meredith was hurt and left the game for good on the next play, and Crow and the Aggies began a savage domination of play that lasted through the final 10 minutes.

Crow was everything that an all-America is supposed to be. He gained 89 yards on 20 carries, got almost all of the yardage on the second (and winning) touchdown drive, intercepted two passes and ran over tacklers all night.

On the game's very first play he started the tide in favor of the Cadets, with a 30-yard kickoff return. An ordinary runner would have been halted by two Mustang tacklers at the 20, but Crow shook them off and kept going to the Aggie 40.

This led to the first A&M touchdown. After the Aggies punted, SMU could not gain, and the Cadets gained

144

Against SMU, John David rushed for 89 yards on 20 carries, intercepted two passes and scored the game-winning TD.

possession on the following punt at the SMU 49.

Eleven plays later, the Aggies scored to take their 6-0 lead.

On the Aggies second touchdown drive, Crow carried the ball on nine of the 14 plays covering the 65 yards and gained 48 of the total yards.

This included some particularly savage running near the SMU goal, with the 215-pound Springhill, La., native gaining 33 of the final 37 yards.

It was in the game's final minutes that Crow made his two interceptions, one blunting an SMU threat at the A&M 20 with the score still 12-6. Crow returned this one four yards to the Aggie 24, and it was from here that A&M launched it game-icing touchdown drive.

He grabbed another one on the final play, taking the ball away from the Mustangs' Billy Dunn at the 20.

He even kicked the extra point after the final A&M touchdown. It was a night of Crow heroics,

so much so that splendid play by Roddy Osborne, alternating at quarterback and halfback for the Aggies, and the fireworks by the Mustangs' Meredith were overshadowed.

The Mustangs had been running from an unbalanced line, first to the right, then to the left, through the first half and the attack was working well under Meredith's pass-run threats.

In the second half, however, the Ponies sprang their spread on the second possession, and gained big yardage with it until Meredith was injured.

The first time it was used, the Mustangs drove from their own 17 to a first down at the A&M 27 before two close calls went against them and the threat failed.

The first one came at about the A&M nine, when a defender knocked down Ray Masters, the Mustang fullback who had gone down field as a receiver. There appeared good reason for an interference call, but the play was ruled as an incomplete pass.

On the next play, Meredith threw a shovel pass forward to Charley Jackson, running back of the line, and the ball fell away from his chest and was covered by Krueger.

The officials ruled it a fumble while Coach Bill Meek of SMU fumed along the sidelines, and after one play was run finally gained an audience with the referee.

The play was ruled a complete forward, then a fumble.

The Aggies' first touchdown drive covered 49 yards on 11 plays, with an important penalty call keeping the Aggies alive.

It came when the Mustangs jumped offside as the Cadets lined up tight on a fourth-down, one-foot to go play at the A&M 39. As the Aggies shifted into a punt formation, half the Mustangs' line chased them and the penalty made it first down. It was the same sort of break that gave life to the Aggies' winning touchdown drive at Fayetteville last week.

Crow chipped in a very big play on this drive by running seven yards to the Pony 3 on first down from the 10.

Loyd Taylor lost a yard, but on the next play, with the Mustangs watching the bruising Crow, Osborne faked to him, kept and circled his own right end for the score.

Taylor's kick was wide.

Meredith got off two good passes, for 17 and 10 yards, on the 12-play, 71-yard drive that tied the score in the second period.

His first toss came after he somehow had evaded Don McClelland, the rushing Aggie and who apparently had the sophomore trapped for a long loss. Meredith connected with Willard Dewveall for 17 yards on this one.

Later in the drive, he tossed a rollout pass to Lon Slaughter for 10 and a first down at the Aggie 16. Other big plays on the drive included a 16-yard run by Slaughter and an 11-yard burst by Wayne Slankard, the Pony fullback.

The payoff was a keeper from the one by Meredith.

As related above, Crow did nearly all the work on the Aggies' second touchdown drive in the third.

The Mustangs helped the Aggies again on their final touchdown drive by jumping offside as the Cadets shifted into punt formation on a fourth-down-and-inches situation. This came at the Aggie 39, the same spot as before, curiously.

A 15-yard roughing penalty against SMU helped A&M on the next play, but the Aggies lost that yardage on a clipping call on still he next play. The penalty against the Aggies partly wiped out a 31-yard run by Charlie Milstead, the A&M sophomore quarterback.

Gordon LeBoeuf, the sophomore fullback, took over here and got most of the remaining yardage, including the final two steps.

Crow, who had done nearly everything else, tried his first extra point this year and made it.

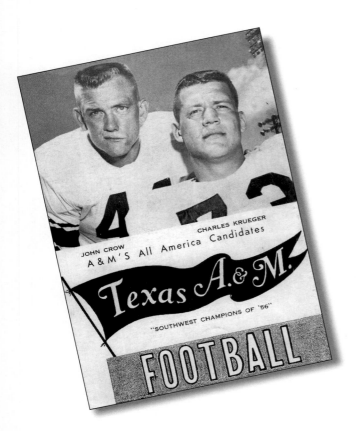

SCORE BY QUARTERS

SMU	0	6	0	0—6
Texas A&M	6	0	6	7—19

Rice Knocks Off No. 1 Aggies, 7-6

By Bill Van Fleet
Fort Worth Star-Telegram

Houston, Nov. 16, 1957

The Texas Aggies fell short of perfection here Saturday and lost their first football game since 1955 as an inspired Rice team handed them a 7-6 defeat.

The fighting Owls seized a 7-0 lead on the second play of the second quarter, finally yielded a touchdown early in the fourth but saw their lead hold at 7-6 when Loyd Taylor's extra point try was wide, and balked the last Aggie threat at the Rice 24 as the clock ran out.

The defeat ended an A&M winning streak at 14 (they were tied by Houston last year) kept them from wrapping up their second successive Southwest Conference title and in all probability knocked them from the No. 1 ranking they have held in the nation's polls.

If the defeat was bitter for Bear Bryant's club, it was a sweet victory for Jess Neely and the Owls.

Rice, loser only to Texas in conference play, now is in position to win the Cotton Bowl bid under its own power if it can beat Texas Christian at Fort Worth next week and Baylor on Nov. 30.

Crowding into the title picture with Rice are the Texas Longhorns, who will meet the Aggies Thanksgiving Day. The Longhorns have lost one and tired one.

King Hill, a great bear of an athlete, was the big man who sealed the Aggies' doom, although still another quarterback, Frank Ryan of Fort Worth, guided the Owl attack to the brink of the Aggie goal on the touchdown drive.

Ryan was hurt as he reached the one-yard line on that drive, and was able to limp into the game for only a brief fourth-period interval before being injured again and removed for good.

But Hill was entirely adequate on the hot, muggy, blustery day that saw a 20-mile wind sweep lengthwise of the gridiron.

The 72,000 fans, the largest turnout in Rice history, were in shirt sleeves as the temperature was 82 degrees.

The 205-pound quarterback from Freeport, a senior taking his last crack at the Aggies, scored the Rice touchdown from the one, carried 13 ties for 43 yards, and completed one pass for nine yards for his offensive chores.

He was more sensational on defense, intercepting two Aggie passes, making numerous tackles and once stopping the Aggies great John David Crow with a clean open field tackle to prevent his breaking into the clear.

His first interception came on the Rice 9-yard line, where he won a three-man battle with the Aggies' Bobby Marks and Larry Dueitt, the sophomore Rice back. He returned to the Rice 21, and from there the

Bobby Joe Conrad (40) hurdles through the grasp of a Rice tackler in search of open field.

first Owl touchdown drive started.

His other interception came at the Aggie 40 in the crucial fourth period as the Cadets were trying desperately for the winning touchdown.

His most important contribution however, may have been when he dropped a 31-yard punt out of bounds on the Aggie one-yard line. This left the Aggies 99 long yards to go against the wind with but

through the humid afternoon. In seven previous games they had averaged 133.9 yards throwing.

Perhaps their strategy was dictated because they never were behind, but arguing against that premise is the fact that they did not pass at all in the scoreless first quarter.

More likely, Neely planned it that way, figuring that the Aggies would be prepared to give his passers a rough time and would cover the star receiver, Buddy Dial, all through the game.

Whether the strategy was preplanned or developed through the course of battle, it worked. The Owls picked up 209 yards rushing over a field left slow by earlier rains, part of it on quarterback keepers that started as if they would be pass plays and most of the rest on quick fullback bursts by the speedy Raymond Chilton and Howard Hoelschor through the middle of the line.

The Aggies won the battle of the statistics, making 17 first downs against 12, and 315 total yards against 218. But the difference o the scoreboard was Hill's extra point.

As for serious threats, the Owls held the edge there, too.

They lost the ball on downs at the Aggie 4 midway in the fourth period when a pass into the end zone was broken up by Taylor, and the limping Ryan failed to make the necessary yard on a fourth-down try from the 31 some

four minutes six seconds to go.

The Aggies kept possession of the ball thereafter, but the clock caught them at the 24, fourth down and 11 yards to go.

The Owls played a game startlingly different from their previous showing, throwing only three passes time later.

The Aggies fought hard, battling to the very final whistle with the spirit that has made them famous through the years, but they were not as sharp and as mistake-free as they had been in their previous seven games this year.

(Above) Fullback Richard Gay (30) powers through the stubborn Rice defense for short yardage.

The extra-point try Taylor missed wasn't the only error for Bryant's team.

When Taylor tried to kick off after that fourth period score, he twice kicked out of bounds and Rice was given the ball at the 50, with the wind at its back. The Aggies never recovered from the hole into which they were thrown.

Even Crow had his troubles. He fumbled at his own 40 in the final seven minutes, and Ryan covered the ball there. This paved the way for Hill's punt out on the A&M 1 that made the distance too great on the Aggies' final drive.

The three interceptions were mentioned earlier, and the Aggie quarterback or ball carriers mishandled the ball six times, losing it to the eager Owls twice.

Part of A&M's bad play had its inception in the hard charging of the Rice line, with Matt Gorges, a senior guard, and Dial and Gene Jones, the starting

(Left) Gordon LeBoeuf (37) snags a high pass from A&M quarterback Jimmy Wright in Rice territory.

ends, particularly alert and rugged.

Gorges made one of those plays a lineman dreams about in the final hectic seconds.

The Aggies were on the Owl 23, second and 10, when Jimmy Wright dropped back to pass. Gorges broke through the A&M defenders, brushed the last blocker aside and threw Wright to the turf for an 11-yard loss back to the 34.

This saved an A&M field goal. There was time for only one more play, and against the wind the new distance was deemed too great.

SCORE BY QUARTERS

Texas A&M	0	0	0	6 —	6
Rice	0	7	0	0 —	7

Lackey's Field Goal Jolts Aggies, 9-7

By Bill Van Fleet
Fort Worth Star-Telegram

College Station, Nov. 28, 1957

By the margin of Bobby Lackey's third-period field goal the Texas Longhorns beat the Texas Aggies, 9-7, in a throbbing, good-to-the-last-second football game.

Victory in this 64th renewal of the famed rivalry leaves Texas with a chance at the Southwest Conference title and almost certainly projected the Longhorns into either the Cotton Bowl, Sugar Bowl or the Gator Bowl.

They finished their conference year with a 4-1-1 record and if Baylor should upset Rice Saturday, they will be conference titlists and the Cotton Bowl team. If Rice and Baylor tie, Texas will be conference co-champion and will get the Cotton Bowl game by virtue of having defeated the Owls earlier in the year.

For the Aggies the game meant bitter disappointment but they likewise are considered possibilities for either the Gator Bowl or the Sugar Bowl.

The Aggies finished with an 8-2 record, having lost their final two games by a margin of three points 7-6 to Rice and 9-7 in this one. Until three weeks ago they were rated No. 1 in the nation.

The capacity crowd of 42,000 saw a brilliantly played football game in near perfect weather — sunny with the temperature hovering in the mid-fifties. A north wind that varied from 10 to 16 mph affected strategy some, but had no real effect on the game. The Longhorns scored a touchdown it the opening quarter on their second possession, moving 33 yards to cross the goal line on eight plays, Lackey got the final foot.

Although the Longhorns moved deep into A&M territory three more times in the first half while keeping the Aggies in their own end of the field, there was no more scoring until Lackey kicked his field goal from the Aggie 28 deep in the third period.

After the half, the Aggies put on a powerful display and moved 80 yards for their score. A towering pass from quarterback Roddy Osborne to all-America John Crow accounted for 57 yards of the move. When Loyd Taylor kicked the point, the importance of Lackey's field goal assumed mountainous proportions.

The Aggie score came with 10 minutes 38 seconds left, and A&M had the wind at its back, but the scrapping Longhorns kept control of the game the rest of the way — although the Aggies were passing desperately and handing out king-size thrills on every play.

The Longhorns won the game with a grinding running attack, one that opened huge holes in the left side of the Aggie line. Even all-America candidate Charlie Krueger on that side couldn't contain the Longhorns.

The Texas team was using an unbalanced line, and in shifting to guard against it the Aggies were leaving a gap in their defense between Krueger and Jim Stanley.

The Texas quarterback, senior Walter Fondren and

sophomore Lackey, pored the sore spot repeatedly send-ing Right halfback Rene Ramirez on dive plays, and trap-ping the situation often to let halfbacks Max Alvis or George Blanch cut back for good yardage.

Then the Longhorns would pull another stunner, with a fake into the right side, then a long, delayed pitchout going to fullback Mike Dowdle, who would go wide.

In all, the hard running accounted for 196 yards, which with 33 more on passes gave Texas a statisti-cal edge of 229 total yards to 218 and a first down margin of 14 to 41.

Texas' biggest edge came on field position, however. Outside the touchdown drive, A&M was in the Longhorns' end of the field only twice — both coming in the third period when they moved against the wind to the Texas 46 one time and to the 31 another time. The first of these mild threats ended on a fourth-down kick and the other on a fumble by Gor-don LeBeouf which was covered by Texas.

BEVO—I'M GONNA BELT YOU—— WHERE IT HURTS.'

McCLANAHAN —

The Longhorns on the other hand, threatened fre-quently. After taking their 6-0 lead, they moved to the Aggie 7 again in the first quarter before A&M held on fourth down.

In the second quarter, they were on the A&M 9 with three downs to go when Fondren fumbled and Darrell Brown covered for A&M. Later in the period, they moved to the 18, but a fine defensive play by Crow that cost Ramirez four yards and a fumble on the next play that Ken Beck covered ended this assault.

Earlier in this drive, Lackey had barely overshot end

Bobby Bryant at the goal on a play that came close to touchdown.

The Texas drive that resulted in the field goal — orig-inated by an Aggie fumble at the A&M 40 was the on-ly penetration into A&M territory in the third period, but the Longhorns moved past midfield twice more in the fourth period, reach-ing the 32 before a holding penalty broke things up on one drive, and at the 43 near the end of the game.

A quick kick by Fon-dren, a weapon that has paid off for Texas all year, set up the first Texas touch-down. The Aggies could move only on short yardage after the opening kickoff was placed at the 20. After three blasts at the Longhorn line Roddy Osborne punt-ed to the Texas 31.

After one running play, Fondren punted 52 yards dead to the Aggie 4.

Three runs for a total of seven yards and Os-borne's short kick into the wind was taken by Fon-dren on the Aggie 34 and returned it one yard.

Eight plays, all on the ground, got the score. Blanch got four, Alvis three, then Blanch cut back on the trap for eight to the 18.

Ramirez ran wide to the left for eight more yards to the 10, and Lackey then made a fine fake before handing to fullback Don Allen, who pounded to the two.

Lackey let Allen get the first yard, then kept twice for the touchdown.

Lackey was back for the extra-point try, but Mickey Smith fumbled the snapback and the Aggies swarmed through before a kick could be attempted, Texas then led 6-0.

Coach Darrell Royal of the Longhorns had to make a pair of big decisions on the field goal that provided the winning points.

The Longhorns had driven from the Aggie 40 to the 22, where it was fourth down and one, with the wind to their backs.

Royal had Fred Bednarski, the kickoff and field goal specialist, ready and eligible to return to the game, and Lackey was calling signals.

First the decision against trying for the first-down yardage was made, then Royal sent Fondren into the game to hold the ball and left Lackey into try for it.

The ball was placed on the 28. Lackey's kick was straight but so low that for a while there was considerable doubt that the ball would clear the crossbar. It did, but with little to spare — and the Longhorns led, 9-0.

Now came the Aggies' touchdown, and it involved the day's most spectacular play — engineered by Osborne and Crow and involving great effort on the part of both.

The Aggies had moved to their own 33 after the kick-off, where it was third down and 7.

Osborne rolled out to the left, shook off tackler after tackler and even pulling away from one who had a grip on his jersey. Finally, he let loose a high, wind-blown pass. Crow took it on the Texas 40, and headed for the goal. He was pulled down by End Monte Lee on the Longhorn 10.

En route he had pulled away from a couple of tacklers.

On the first play from the 10, Monte Lee broke through to pin a four-yard loss on Crow, but on the next play the 215-pound Aggie fought, dug, and twisted his way for 12 yards to the two, where it was third down.

Osborne kept for a yard, making it fourth and one. Crow got the final yard on a dive. Taylor kicked the extra point.

Now began a race with the clock. There was 10:38 left, and Texas got the ball at its own 20.

Lackey guided the team on a 48-yard, time-consuming drive before a holding penalty halted them. It came on first down and wiped out a seven-yard gain by Blanch and set the Longhorns back in the A&M 47.

A couple of plays later Allen Goehring covered a fumble by Alvis at the Aggie 47, and the big crowd came to its feet.

A fiery Texas pass defense swarmed after Osborne and his substitute, Charlie Milstead. On the third play, Henry Anderson, the Texas guard and linebacker, intercepted a Milstead pass at the Texas 44.

Three plays failed to get a first down, and Fondren came in to kick. He sent a high punt into the wind and Crow took it on a fair catch at the 17.

There was 1:55 left and now Texas sent six men into the secondary, one in a regular safety position to guard against the kind of pass that ha set up the A&M touchdown earlier.

Don Smith dropped the first Milstead pass, but Crow took a pitchout, then threw a running pass that got 16 yards to the Aggie 33.

Milstead with the crowd roaring, passed incomplete when rushed badly, then handed to Taylor on a draw play that got six yards.

Milstead lost four yards as he tripped over a teammate, but on fourth down passed to Smith for 11 yards and a first down at the 45.

There were 31 seconds left now.

Big Larry Stephens, the Texas end, got Milstead for a four-yard loss, and after that Milstead threw an incomplete pass that stopped the clock with two seconds left.

Milstead got away with another pass on the final play, but Texas fullback Jim Welch ran under it at about the Texas 40 and returned to midfield as the game ended.

SCORE BY QUARTERS

Texas	6	0	3	0—9
Texas A&M	0	0	0	7—7

Royal Built Better 'Bear' Trap and Bryant's Boys Took the Bait

By Gene Gregston
Fort Worth Star-Telegram

Y ou might say the Texas longhorns built a better trap for Texas A&M here. A three-play series from an unbalanced line laid the solid foundation upon which the Orange constructed the 9-7 upset of the Aggies.

"The Aggie trap," and the "Aggie pitch" were designations for two of the maneuvers, while the complementing move from the formation was a halfback dive.

The trap and dive crucified the left defensive side of the Cadets defense, while the pitch off the trap series sent the Texas fullbacks, Mike Dowdle or Don Allen, springing wide to the right.

"That was thought up by Darrell (Coach Darrell Royal)," said Longhorn assistant Charles Shira. "He's got a fertile mind."

Fertile is right. The innovation blossomed, beautifully into what the Longhorns' young head tutor described as the most satisfying victory of his career.

The groundwork for the stunning surprise was laid in two ways by Texas' repeated running to the weak side of the formation against Rice in the only previous game the Longhorns have used the unbalanced line to a great extent, and scouting reports which showed the Aggies adjusting little to the strong side.

Texas coaches anticipated the Cadets "staying home" to protect against the weak side. They guessed correctly.

"Another reason for it," said Shira, "was their linebacker Dick Gay. He's made 75 percent of their tackles this year and we had to find something to give him a misdirection."

Television screens may have shown the field goal which supplied the winning points, but they possibly could not convey the intricacy of this new formation.

Royal explained how it worked. On the trap play, Wilson or Anderson would pull and go across and knock the Aggies' Charlie Krueger out as he charged in. Robert E. Lee and Garland Kennon, James Shillingburg, and Will Wyman two-timed Jim Stanley or Buddy Payne to the inside.

J.T. Seaholm and Wyman angled to the left and cut down Gay, or his replacement. Into the gap between Krueger and Stanley would fly Texas left halfbacks George Blanch and Max Alvis, who alternated at the position when Alvis wasn't at right half.

Quarterback Walter Fondren and Bobby Lackey would either give to the right halfback, Rene Ramirez or Alvis, on the straight-ahead dive at the gap; give to Blanch or Alvis on the slant at the gap; or fake to Blanch or Alvis and then pitch to Dowdle or Allen going wide to the outside.

The Aggies never could bring themselves to concentrate their defense against the series. Sometimes Stanley would move outside farther and Gay would pull over, but the Longhorns still had them outnumbered and outblocked.

Texas offensive line coach Jim Pittman said simply, "that won it for us."

155

Richard Gay (30) eludes a Vol tackler
while darting off-tackle.

Tennessee Noses Out Aggies, 3-0

By Gene Gregston
Fort Worth Star-Telegram

Jacksonville, Fla., Dec. 27, 1957

The Gator Bowl, "where touchdowns (used to) reign," was almost a pointless embarrassment on its 13th annual renewal here this gray day.

But a fourth-string fullback, Sammy Burklow, kicked a short field goal in the final period to give Tennessee a well-earned 3-0 triumph over Texas A&M.

A crowd of 43,709 — a new record attendance — watched the anticipated hard-hitting contest unfold on a field made muddy by morning showers.

They saw little of excitable nature other than an 82-yard punt return by Vol tailback Bobby Gordon, which was nullified by a clipping penalty, and Burklow's kick, which climaxed the game's best drive of 49 yards.

The 200-pound junior from Hazard, Ky., who makes game appearances only for kickoffs, extra points and field goals, kicked from the Aggies' 7-yard line with 5½ minutes remaining. The line of scrimmage was the A&M 1, and there was only a slight angle to the flight of the ball.

It was practically duck soup for Burklow, although this was his — and Tennessee's first field goal attempt of the 1957 season. He kicked 17 of 19 extra point attempts during the regular campaign — the two failures were blocked.

Gordon, who was voted the Vols' most valuable player — John Crow won the honor on the losing side —

had been instrumental in carrying the single-wing attack into field-goal position.

The tailback passed to wingback Bill Anderson for 19 yards, hurled to end Landon Darty for nine, and ran for 12 yards in the big plays from the 50 to the one.

There, faced with a fourth-down decision as to kick or go for the touchdown, Tennessee hazarded a guess on the boy from Hazard.

Burklow's field goal capped a second-half Volunteer domination so complete the Aggies netted only 47 yards and two first downs after intermission.

A&M had held the upper hand the first half, but neither team came any closer than 30 yards of scoring in those two opening quarters, discounting Gordon's great run that was erased.

Tennessee moved to the A&M 14 and 27 in the third quarter, but was halted by first-down fumbles each time. Those were the game's most serious scoring threats other than Burklow's successful kick.

Gordon and Crow were the workhorses. Gordon set a new Gator Bowl record for caries 32 times for 60 yards. Crow netted 46 on 14 tries.

SCORE BY QUARTERS

Tennessee	0	0	0	3—3
Texas A&M	0	0	0	0—0

CAREER STATISTICS

At Texas A&M

	RUSHING			RECEIVING			SCORING	
	Att.	Yds.	Avg.	No.	Yds.	Avg.	TD	Pts.
1955	66	352	5.0	5	101	20.2	4	24
1956	101	561	5.6	6	117	19.5	12	72
1957	129	562	4.4	2	62	31.0	6	37
Total	**296**	**1,455**	**4.9**	**13**	**280**	**21.5**	**22**	**132**

At Chicago and St. Louis Cardinals

	RUSHING			RECEIVING			SCORING	
	Att.	Yds.	Avg.	No.	Yds.	Avg.	TD	Pts.
1958	52	221	4.3	20	362	18.1	6	36
1959	140	666	4.8	27	328	12.1	7	42
1960	181	1,071	5.9	25	462	18.5	9	54
1961	48	192	4.0	20	306	15.3	4	24
1962	192	751	3.9	23	246	10.7	17	102
1963	9	34	3.8	0	0	0	0	0
1964	163	554	3.4	23	257	11.7	8	48
Total	**785**	**3,489**	**4.3**	**138**	**1,961**	**12.3**	**51**	**306**

At San Francisco 49ers

	RUSHING			RECEIVING			SCORING	
	Att.	Yds.	Avg.	No.	Yds.	Avg.	TD	Pts.
1965	132	514	3.9	28	493	17.6	9	54
1966	121	477	3.9	30	341	11.4	4	24
1967	113	479	4.2	31	373	12.0	5	30
1968	4	4	1.0	31	531	17.1	5	30
Total	**370**	**1,474**	**4.0**	**120**	**1,738**	**14.5**	**23**	**138**

BIOGRAPHIES

ABOUT THE AUTHOR

Steve Pate is a freelance writer who spent 20 years as a sports writer with The Fort Worth Star-Telegram, The Dallas Morning News, The New York Post and The National.

In 1993, he was a recipient of the J. Frank Dobie Piasano Literary Fellowship at the University of Texas.

A resident of Dallas, he recently co-authored Matt Martnez's *Culinary Frontier: A Real Texas Cookbook* with Matt Martinez Jr.

ABOUT THE EDITOR

Dan Jenkins is one of America's most renowned sports writers. Jenkins is the author of more than a dozen books, including the bestsellers, *Semi-Tough* (1972), *Dead Solid Perfect* (1974), *Limo* (1976), *Baja Oklahoma* (1981), *Life It's Own Self* (1984), *Fast Copy* (1988), and *You Gotta Play Hurt* (1991).

A native of Fort Worth and an alumnus of TCU, Jenkins' most enjoyable boyhood memories are having watched Sam Baugh and Davey O'Brien lead the Horned Frogs to national championships in 1935 and 1938.

John David Crow (left), his wife, Carolyn (right), and family.